Deepening **Faith**

Dealing with **Doubts**

Coping with **Trials**

Getting **Assurance**

PETER MASTERS

Wakeman Trust, London

FAITH, DOUBTS, TRIALS AND ASSURANCE

THE WAKEMAN TRUST
(Wakeman Trust is a UK Registered Charity)

UK Registered Office
38 Walcot Square
London SE11 4TZ

US Office
300 Artino Drive
Oberlin, OH 44074-1263
Web site: www.wakemantrust.org

ISBN 1 870855 50 7

ISBN-13 978 1 870855 50 1

Cover design by Andrew Owen

Printed by Stephens & George, Merthyr Tydfil, UK

Contents

Deepening Faith

– PART ONE –

1

Testing Our Level of Faith

'Wherefore, if God so clothe the grass of the field, which today is, and tomorrow is cast into the oven, shall he not much more clothe you, O ye of little faith?' ***(Matthew 6.30.)***

TO POSSESS only a small degree of faith is a major catastrophe for Christian believers, because faith is central and crucial to the spiritual life and the key to proving the Lord. This chapter is not about saving faith, but the *ongoing* faith which is essential for answered prayer, effective service, spiritual stability, and real communion with Christ. What a sad situation it is when our faith must be described by our Saviour as 'little faith', a feeble, shrivelled, diminutive trust in Him.

Once we are saved we cannot lose our salvation but we shall certainly miss the full enjoyment and power of salvation if our faith has withered through not being exercised. The Lord's term 'little faith' should alarm us into checking the state of our 'belief-system', the liveliness of our trust. The Lord did not do many mighty works in Capernaum because of lack of faith among the people, and how can our lives be blessed with instrumentality, spiritual insight and joy in the Lord if we lack living, active faith?

In many passages of Scripture we are shown that faith is vital to blessing, such as *Matthew 9.22*, where we read those familiar words of the Lord, 'Daughter, be of good comfort; thy faith hath made thee whole.' A few verses later we hear Him say, 'According to your faith be it unto you,' and again, in *Luke 7.50,* He says to another woman – 'Thy faith hath saved thee.' Similarly, to the blind beggar in *Luke 18.42,* Christ says, 'Thy faith hath saved thee,' repeatedly emphasising the necessity of active faith in the securing of blessing. What a blessing it is to have the opposite of little faith seen in *Matthew 15.28* – 'Then Jesus answered and said unto her, O woman, great is thy faith: be it unto thee even as thou wilt. And her daughter was made whole from that very hour.'

How do we define ongoing faith? Faith means to be fully and completely persuaded and convinced of the reality of God's existence and character, and of the infallibility of all His acts, words and promises, so that we wholly trust our lives and our affairs to Him. There is always some faith in believers, and because this is so we too easily imagine that our faith is healthy. Even a cold and somewhat backslidden believer will give correct answers to doctrinal questions, showing that *theoretical* belief is alive and well, and yet *active* faith may be in very poor shape. Such a person will not be living as though he really believes the things he affirms. It may be, for example, that when plunged into a crisis, calamity or problem, he goes to pieces, panics, and becomes utterly dejected, making no attempt to seriously pray and submit the matter to God. This is an obvious and common example of how someone may believe intellectually, but lose all practical application of faith to the affairs of life.

If, under test, we do not take the steps which the Bible prescribes, it is because our faith has shrivelled, and this happens to pastors as well as all other Christians. Even stalwart, long-standing believers may experience through sin or neglect a dramatic loss of active faith.

Faith is rather like the muscles of the body – always there, but often in poor condition because nothing is done to preserve fitness. In life we may become desk-bound, losing the energy and stamina we need to cope with extra demands. If not exercised faith also runs down rapidly so that the devil can defeat us with great ease. The analogy of faith and bodily fitness applies even more to mature Christians than to young ones. A young, inexperienced Christian may possess a more lively faith than a seasoned believer, just as young people may enjoy much greater bodily fitness than their elders, possessing a physical elasticity and durability which has deserted those who are only a few years ahead of them. Similarly, as the Christian life proceeds the muscles of faith can become enfeebled, leaving people far more vulnerable to doubt and cynicism, whereas the young believer may still be close enough to conversion to trust the Lord in any situation. It is therefore vital as we grow older in the faith that we take care to exercise and cultivate faith.

Faith is Not Executive Power

At this point it must be stressed that the Bible does not speak of faith as having executive power. This is the kind of faith claimed by most charismatics who say that if you want to be healed you must pray the 'prayer of faith', meaning you must pray with absolute certainty and confidence and then you will be healed. They teach that if faith has the right quality and strength it virtually possesses executive power to summon down the power of God. Some charismatic teachers go so far as to tell people to imagine or visualise the desired answer, and to praise and thank God as though it had already been received.

This notion of faith is wrong, because true faith recognises that God alone is sovereign, and He knows His wise will and purpose for each of His people. When we pray for a blessing such as healing God will answer according to His wonderful wisdom and perfect plan for us, which may not be what we expect. We know that He is ready to be entreated by His people because He has said so, but it often happens that our desires are not in line with His sovereign purpose, and that He has a better way, therefore it is not right for the believer to work up an artificial emotional certainty about the outcome of a situation as though he could dominate God.*

The true prayer of faith amounts to this: we plead with God (for legitimate things) totally persuaded that if He chooses to bring these things to pass He will have no difficulty. The prayer of faith believes that the Lord has all the necessary power, and that He is ready to hear the cries of His people. The prayer of faith also accepts that God's sovereign and wonderful wisdom will prevail. Genuine biblical faith is a firm belief that whatever the Lord does, and however He disposes of the case, will be perfect.

God loves faith in His people because it serves so many purposes. It *glorifies* God, focusing our minds upon His power, and it also *appreciates* Him, keeping our eyes upon His kindness, goodness and promises. Faith expresses dependence, admiration, and humble, unreserved acceptance of God's will, causing us to suppress human pride and to pray constantly for all our blessing. It is the absolute conviction that in all circumstances we need the smile and blessing of God or we shall fail in every spiritual aim. In this way faith sees and grasps reality, for when we are full of faith we see ourselves as

*Charismatic teachers appeal to *Mark 11.22-24* in support of their definition of the 'prayer of faith', but our Lord's words must be interpreted in the light of such passages as *Mark 14.36* and *James 4.15.* Scripture cannot contradict itself, and these other passages call us to recognise and bow to the superior wisdom and will of God in all things. *Mark 11.22-24* is first and foremost an instruction to the disciples as future apostles. They would frequently receive special directions from the Spirit to heal or to perform some other sign, and under these unmistakable circumstances they were to pray and act in total certainty of faith. In our case, however, the certainty of faith applies whenever we pray for those things which are unconditionally promised by God to His people, such as forgiveness by the blood of Christ, God's help in the fight against sin, ability to witness and grace to bear persecution and trial. But for matters which are not specifically and unconditionally promised, such as healing, we pray subject to the unknown will of God, as *James 4.15* prescribes.

small, needy and insufficient, and we respect and feel our need of the power of God.

When Faith Runs Down

The loss of faith is the high road to spiritual disaster as we see from the Lord's words to Peter, recorded in *Luke 22.31-32*, 'Simon, Simon, behold, Satan hath desired to have you, that he may sift you as wheat: but I have prayed for thee, that thy faith fail not.' Satan has the same aim for all of us, working to reduce us to the point where he can do anything he wants with us. In the case of Peter, he attacked his faith until he no longer believed the Lord could deliver him, and then came the shameful moment when the Lord was denied. Faith is always under attack from the devil. He wants to make us complacent, self-reliant and prayerless, no longer putting spiritual matters first in our lives. He aims to stop us proving the Lord and make us afraid to represent Him in the world. If Satan can bring down our faith, he can succeed in these objectives.

Tragically, when faith declines, we are usually unaware how bad matters have become. Peter said, 'Lord, I am ready to go with thee, both into prison, and to death,' but the Saviour knew that his faith was in a low condition and about to fail. We may sometimes think that we have suffered no great attacks from Satan for some while, not having been tempted to doubt the faith or to question our salvation, or to commit any *great* sin, but if we examined ourselves honestly we may find that earnest prayer has diminished and satisfaction with earthly things has grown. If the devil is quiet on the more prominent matters we may be sure that he is undermining the constant, active exercise of faith, because he never stops attacking this.

The words of Christ to Peter teach us that feelings can greatly mislead us, for Peter felt spiritually strong and buoyant, so much so that he was confident he would stand up to martyrdom. His feelings were warm and fervent, but under testing his faith quickly collapsed.

Sometimes with us it is the other way round, because our feelings simply do not function as they should, and we feel spiritually cold, making praise and prayer a struggle. We fear that we are backslidden, but although feelings have failed, faith may be strong. Strong feelings with weak faith will, as with Peter, let us down, but weak feelings accompanied by strong faith will win through. Of course, it is best to have both, but if we ever have to choose between them for a time, let us aim at strong faith, because this matters most of all.

Measuring Faith

The state or condition of our faith may be measured fairly well by a few questions, the first of which is – How much do we pray privately? If we spend little time in secret prayer it is a sure indication that our active faith is low because evidently we do not see much purpose in praying. Prayer has ceased to be important because we have lost any deep apprehension of the power and goodness of God, we are no longer aware that He watches us, and no longer feel that He can do great things for us. We may be fully persuaded of the faith intellectually, but at the practical level we are no longer strongly convinced about these things. If we were, we would be anxious about yesterday's lack of prayer, but we are not, and so today's prayer will be allowed to slip also.

We feel no fear, no insecurity, and no sense of impending failure or chastisement by the Lord, because we no longer believe that God is offended by our coldness and self-reliance. We do not feel that we need take seriously the biblical warnings about prayerlessness. We are no longer deeply *convinced* and *persuaded* about such spiritual realities, meaning that our faith is dwindling to almost nothing.

A second test-question to determine the state of our faith is to ask what we do first when trouble strikes. How do we react under trial or when in pain or difficulty? To what do we turn for relief? If our immediate reaction is to go to pieces, to lose our temper, or to strike out in some way with hostile and bitter thoughts or words against the imagined cause of our woes (or those unfortunate enough to be around us) then the signs are bad. Or if we run away from the situation and bury our head in some worldly entertainment, then active faith is clearly in poor shape. If our reaction to trouble is anything other than to pray and to trust the promises and providential oversight of the Lord, it shows that our faith has atrophied to a low condition.

A third test-question for the quality of our faith examines the nature or character of our prayers, asking – What are our prayers like? Was yesterday's prayer the same as that of today, and so on back through the previous week and even the previous month? If our prayers are always much the same, being mechanical and formal in character, then it is a sad but sure indication that our faith is small and poor. It indicates that we are not currently convinced of our need of God's help in all our circumstances. We are no longer persuaded that prayer is essential before the work of our church can be blessed, or that we have a duty to make intercession for others. Because we are no longer fully persuaded about these things, we cannot be bothered to bring fresh, different, strongly needed matters before the Lord each day. Our praying vigour and variation has evaporated because deep down we are no longer certain that prayer makes much difference.

A fourth and allied question would be to ask how much prayer we put behind the service of the Lord, because our answer will again reveal whether we really think prayer is worthwhile. If we had strong faith and were certain that prayer moves the Spirit to melt hearts and regenerate souls, then we would never neglect our appeals to God. The problem is never shortage of time for prayer, but a lack of persuasion or conviction that prayer is essential, pleasing to God, and instrumental in obtaining the blessing.

A fifth useful test-question might be to ask whether we still *enjoy* the things of God, deriving great pleasure from the Word, the service of the Gospel and the proving of the Lord. A low level of happiness in spiritual things is a sure sign of a low level of faith, for when we are convinced about the wonderful things of God we cannot help being thrilled and warmed by them. In *Philippians 1.25* Paul says – 'I know that I shall abide and continue with you all for your furtherance and joy of faith.' Active faith here is linked with progress and enjoyment, for it brings tremendous spiritual pleasure. So how depleted is our faith? How urgently does it need repair and revitalisation? If the test-questions suggested here lead to discouragement, the next chapter proposes remedial steps for the rebuilding of faith.

2

Eight Ways to Strengthen Faith

'We are bound to thank God always for you, brethren, as it is meet, because that your faith groweth exceedingly' *(2 Thessalonians 1.3).*

FOR THE LIFELONG EFFORT of keeping and developing active personal faith, we need to know which activities are faith-strengthening and which are faith-weakening. Contrary to what we would naturally like, the most effective environment for the strengthening of faith is provided by trials, permitted by the Lord in order that we should cast ourselves upon His help, and prove His promises *(James 1.2-3* and *2 Corinthians 12.7-10)*. If we react well to these there will also be spiritual benefit for those around us, both believers and unbelievers, as they see us stand up to our problems maintaining Christian character, love and unselfishness. We remember that it was through trials and weaknesses that the trust of the apostle Paul grew to the point where he could say, 'Most gladly therefore will I rather glory in my infirmities, that the power of Christ may rest upon me.'

If trials are faith-strengthening the opposite is often true of times of ease and prosperity, or of good health and strong capability. If not handled properly these may serve to be faith-weakening by producing self-reliance and spiritual complacency. No doubt this is why the Lord seldom permits such times to last for long before we are touched by some kind of hardship. If we enjoy a long season of success in all departments of life, coupled with fine health, the best action we can take to maintain strong faith is to give ourselves to a really challenging avenue of service for the Lord, because this will bring us to need His special help. A good pastor should have the very task waiting to be carried out, and then a double blessing may be had, the blessing of needy souls through our labours, and our own proving of the Lord and growth in faith.

Aside from seasons of trial there are a number of faith-strengthening activities, and we now list eight of these. This list does not include obvious and basic 'strengtheners' such as regular prayer and the devotional study of God's Word.

1. Daily Praise and Gratitude

An essential and infallible faith-strengthener is to praise the Lord for Who He is, and for His works, sincerely and frequently. The practice of also recognising the hand of the Lord in the events of life, reflecting on His goodness, and expressing gratitude in detail, considerably deepens love, loyalty and trust. This is made clear from the prayers of the Bible, which extol and praise Almighty God first, and then make petitions. *Ephesians 1.15-19* provides the following example of praise-rich prayer:

> **'Wherefore I also, after I heard of your faith in the Lord Jesus, and love unto all the saints, cease not to give thanks for you, making mention of you in my prayers; that the God of our Lord Jesus Christ, the Father of glory, may give unto you the spirit of wisdom and revelation in the knowledge of him: the eyes of your understanding being enlightened; that ye may know what is the hope of his calling, and what the riches of the glory of his inheritance in the saints, and**

> **what is the exceeding greatness of his power to us-ward who believe, according to the working of his mighty power.'**

Other great thanksgiving prayers include *Psalm 103, Acts 4.23-30,* and *Colossians 1.3-12.*

A feeble spirit of gratitude soon collapses before the invading forces of self-pity, grumbling, and coldness – all of which are expressions of faithlessness. Daily and fervent praise is not only God's right, but it is essential nourishment to our own faith. Every day our debt of gratitude must be properly and worthily paid so that He receives the glory. (We say more about praise and thanksgiving in chapter 10.)

2. Diligent Use of Memory

A second faith-strengthener is to exercise and employ the memory for recalling and recounting great answers to prayer, major deliverances, and other interventions of the Lord in our lives. Forgetfulness is near to treachery, while an expansive memory-bank of divine blessing is the very energy of faith, and from earliest times God's people have realised this. From Bethel's pillar, Jordan's memorial stones, and Samuel's Ebenezer, to the Saviour's ordinances of baptism and breaking of bread, the lesson is repeatedly taught – remember the wonderful works of God. If we had well-stocked memories of blessing we would not be cast down so easily by passing distresses, but would come sooner and more trustingly to the throne of grace. Our memories tend instead to hoard heaps of irrelevant bric-a-brac, all crowding out priceless evidences of God's goodness and power towards us. If the memory is poor the believer should keep a diary of blessing and consult it often, especially in times of trial.

Our testimony of salvation should be recalled from time to time, and if possible anniversaries of significant blessings kept for personal prayer. We should never be content with vague and general thanksgiving, but should spell out our blessings with wonder, love and rejoicing. We should never generalise or trivialise the gracious, powerful, wise and loving acts of our God toward us, for to generalise is to minimise, and to minimise is eventually to take for granted and forget. The way we use our memory is either greatly strengthening or greatly weakening to personal faith.

3. Enthusiasm for the Cause

A third sure faith-strengthener is to focus the mind and interests on the Lord's work, not only by helping in some significant form of Christian service, but also by being an avid follower of spiritual events. How are all the departments in the church getting on? What is the Lord doing? What should I pray for? Who are the new people in my fellowship, and is there any part I can play in encouraging them? What is the news from missionaries, church planters and other members working at a distance from our congregation? How are this year's special church projects progressing? Our church – our colony or outpost of Heaven on earth – should be our life, our love and our calling, and this is where the Lord intends our 'earthly' attention to be concentrated, not on personal and trivial earthly things and small-talk. The work of the Spirit and triumphs of grace in and through the churches should mean everything to us. A verse of Isaac Watts describes so accurately the attitude of a heart devoted to Christ:–

Thou art the source of love
Whence all my pleasures flow;
The sphere in which my interests move,
And all my hopes below.

In the Bible faith is always inextricably linked with viewing and proving the things of God. It is a virtue which lives and thrives on spiritual issues, and withers away if forced to survive on a diet of earthly affairs. If we are absorbed by the 'good fight of faith', the noble contest for Truth and for souls, then our faith will be activated and deepened, because spiritual interests reinforce our sense of the reality of God's mission and purpose in the world. Earthly, secular interests, on the other hand, draw the mind and heart away from these realities, undermining faith.

Do we take an interest in the wider spiritual battle, concerned to know how the devil is currently attacking Bible-believing, Gospel-preaching churches around the world? What form does his offensive currently take, to infiltrate and compromise God's people? What are the agencies, organisations and periodicals which encourage and promote Satan's latest schemes, and who are the spokesmen who strive to protect the people of God and call them back to the old paths? Who needs our special encouragement and our prayers?

Perhaps a believer is oblivious to the battle going on around him, taking no interest in the wider scene. Perhaps a child of God has very little idea what is really happening even in his own church, being too absorbed by his own world. How can a 'switched-off', unmoved, uninvolved person whose spiritual engagement has languished, have healthy faith? We must take steps to stir up and maintain a passionate interest in the spiritual warfare.

Anything of this world that takes too much of our emotional energy and leisure time should be curbed, for it steals our interest in the work and the people of God. Some believers become infatuated with radio and television programmes and need to severely ration their intake and be much more selective. Others need to control their passion for over-decorating their homes, or for giving excessive time to other earthly obsessions. Is our conversation solely about the pressures at work, the family, and secular events, or is it all about money and the car and the home and babies (wonderful as they are) and shopping and cooking? Do we not realise that it is the devil's aim, to limit us to earthly affairs, not the Lord's aim? It is Satan who steers our minds and our talk to concentrate on earthly things, and who strips us of all elevated, grand, and expansive spiritual interests. Faith needs a broader outlook, an interested mind, an inquisitive mind, and a mind in business for the Lord. It thrives in a mind which discerns the times, follows the battle, and is alert to spiritual events. It grows in those whose interest in such matters is unquenchable and who come regularly before the Lord in prayer. Such an interest in spiritual news and affairs is a powerful faith-strengthener.

4. Pursuit of Sanctification

A fourth faith-strengthener is a conscientious application to personal sanctification. *Hebrews* chapter 11, one of the best known of all biblical passages on faith, reaches its climax in *Hebrews 12.1*: 'Wherefore seeing we also are compassed about with so great a cloud of witnesses, let us lay aside every weight, and the sin which doth so easily beset us, and let us run with patience the race that is set before us.' These words show that faith and the zealous pursuit of holiness go hand in hand, for according to *Hebrews 11*, faith was the glory of men who kept apart from the sin of the society around them. We learn that lively, active faith cannot flourish in a believer unless the war against personal sin is being strenuously conducted.

Throughout the Bible, whenever God's people abandoned holiness, their faith failed. Therefore, to preserve and increase faith, we must examine ourselves daily to identify and regret our sin, sincerely repent of it, and promise the Lord that we will fight to avoid it. All this is essential to maintain our relationship with God, secure His presence and power in our lives, and have assurance revived.

We may easily trace the way in which active faith is reduced by lack of self-examination and repentance. In order to neglect repentance we have to think that it does not matter and that God does not greatly notice or mind our sin. We have to take the view that no harm will come to us and that God will bless us just the same. In the last resort we have to feel that if the Lord does withdraw from us, we will survive reasonably well, and soon time will obliterate all memory of our sin and all will be well. In other words, to neglect repentance and holiness I must become a kind of 'unbelieving believer' who no longer takes the Lord (or His warnings) particularly seriously. I must reach the point where I am no longer alarmed at my neglect, and do not fear any consequences or tremble at the Word. *Psalm 36* describes such a person saying, 'There is no fear of God before his eyes,' and this is the psychology behind the neglect of personal sanctification and the undermining of faith or belief. Great conscientiousness is therefore an essential faith-preserver and strengthener, while slackness is a destructive weakener.

The counsel we need for building faith is never to repent in vague or general terms, without a feeling of shame and a genuine desire to do better, and never to let a day pass without clearing the debt of sin. These are the most important steps that we can take, for they restore peace with God, and re-ignite the fires of faith.

5. Respect for Providence

A fifth faith-strengthener is the practice of respecting and accepting the overruling providences of God in our lives with reverence, peace and acceptance. We should always recognise that there is a higher plan and purpose in all our circumstances, good and bad, whether the house has been burgled, or redundancy has struck, or any other kind of disturbance or illness has entered life. No event is an unnecessary, unplanned occurrence, and no difficulty is a pointless blow, justifying an angry, frustrated response from us. If we see ourselves as helpless corks bobbing on the surface of a great ocean, the victims of random waves, we virtually throw away the faculty of faith.

It is an essential faith-strengthener that we learn to step back and to think in the context of God's superintendency of our lives, because there is always a gracious providence at work in the lives of Christians. The unexpected happens because the sovereign Guardian of my soul has permitted it. He Who has loved me, saved me, and kept me up till now knows all about it, for I am never out of His sight and will and training and protective power, and He knows what good He will bring from it. Indeed, the Lord planned and permitted all the rigours of my journey before the foundation of the world, and His perfect wisdom is in them all.

In my problem, I ask, am I experiencing a correction for sin or foolishness or neglect of spiritual duties? Or is there something new for me to learn? Or is this problem a new, unenvisaged opportunity to testify to the goodness of God before other people? Is some aspect of Christian character about to be developed in me, through changed circumstances? Am I about to find myself trained for a new avenue of service? If I respect God's providence and remember the operation of God's overruling power, humble awe will replace bitterness and pain, and the distressed mind will be lifted above the present and may even catch a glimpse of His grand scheme. (A more detailed treatment of this profound subject follows in Part Three of this book.) To respect and rejoice in God's providential superintendency of life is a magnificent faith-strengthener.

6. Unselfish Demeanour

A sixth faith-strengthener is the practice of giving out rather than just taking in. We must aim to be those who minister to and help others, firstly because it is God's will for us, and secondly because this is a stance which builds up faith. It was the stance of Christ, and the more we resemble Him, the more faith will flourish in us. The express command of the Lord and the most conspicuous mark of discipleship is that we love one another *(John 13.34-35)*, which means showing affection to one another, giving preference to one another, serving one another, extending kindness to one another, edifying one another, praying for one another, and being hospitable to one another *(Romans 12.10; Galatians 5.13; Ephesians 4.32; 1 Thessalonians 5.11; James 5.16; 1 Peter 4.9)*.

To outgoing love we add the lifestyle of *Romans 12*, where Paul directs that we present our bodies as a living sacrifice, committed to the cause of the Gospel, to lost souls and to other believers. This is the only lifestyle which reflects the life of Christ and obeys His will, and this alone is consistent with faith. If we really and deeply believe God, we will want to do things His way. *Philippians 2.4* exhorts: 'Look not every man on his own things, but every man also on the things of others.' If we reject this exhortation as the rule of our lives, then we have already suppressed active belief in God's revealed will for us.

'Selfism', or being preoccupied with ourselves, is a ruthless enemy of faith, causing us to be governed by our own fortunes, happiness, reputation and future, taking us out of step and out of sympathy with the Lord, and making us unusable by Him in the blessing of others. If, on the other hand, we are concerned for others and for the Gospel we will pray for blessing upon our words and actions, God will use us, and we will enjoy a stream of faith-strengthening evidence of His power.

We need constantly to be asking ourselves what we could be doing for this or that person, or what conversation we should be starting, or what encouragement or kindness we should be showing. The believer who lives according to this unselfish, outgoing, ever-imparting, ever-helping rule, and who develops an outgoing disposition, will unquestionably grow in faith, because he imitates Christ.

7. Thoughtful Worship

A seventh faith-strengthener is the practice of worshipping with mind and heart together, our tendency being to use one faculty without the other, or to use both with great disparity. In the singing of hymns, for example, believers may notice only the most obvious evangelical sentiments, clothing them with gratitude to God and winging them heavenward. However, there may be only shallow appreciation of deeper matters in the hymns, and this curtails faith because faith is based on intelligently appreciated facts. Faith needs all the truths of the faith as well as love to function properly and grow. 'I will sing with the spirit,' says Paul, 'and I will sing with the understanding also' *(1 Corinthians 14.15)*, and in saying this he echoes *Psalm 47.7* – 'Sing ye praises with understanding.'

The Lord said – 'They that worship him must worship him in spirit and in truth' *(John 4.24)*, showing that we should worship with our whole soul, and especially with understanding of spiritual truth. The mind as well as the emotions must be committed to God in worship, and feelings of gratitude, love and joy must flow from a solid mental grasp of the great doctrines of the faith, of the work of Christ, and of spiritual blessings. If ministers select hymns which teem with doctrinal inaccuracies and vague or obscure sentiments, then congregations will develop the habit of appropriating only the gist of those hymns in their worship. Similarly, if hymns state only the simplest truths in shallow terms, then believers will learn to praise with only half their minds. To sing hymns worthily requires the selection of credible hymns so that worshippers may value the lines for their meaning, reflect on them and mean them fully. Line by line the mind must be engaged, then the deeper emotions of the soul will be moved not merely by the 'gist' and the melody but by full appreciation of grand, deep statements about the Lord and His ways. Many of the hymn sentiments and prayers offered in worship take the form of affirmation of doctrines, the hearty affirmation of Truth being an essential exercise of faith.

It is sad to observe that some believers habitually sing hymns like traumatised or exhausted people, not appearing to engage mind and spirit at all. They seem not to have discovered that worship offered with all one's faculties and effort brings us near to God, and Him to us, and that this is gloriously faith-strengthening. Worship that is thoughtful and feelingful strengthens faith in a unique manner.

8. Firm Self-discipline

An eighth faith-strengthener, often unrecognised as such but essential, is the practice of self-discipline. 'Fight the good fight of faith' says Paul *(1 Timothy 6.12)*, and in describing the Christian's fight he speaks of 'the shield of faith' *(Ephesians 6.16)*. Paul's 'fight' is a parallel figure to his running of the race, which involved keeping under his body and bringing it into subjection, this language of self-discipline being found in *1 Corinthians 9.27.* Faith is greatly exercised in the battle against sin, especially in the struggle with our own fleshly nature. The impulsive, 'floppy' person, who asserts little self-control or self-government, will never possess strong faith, and sadly there are many undisciplined believers who allow their muscles of self-control to become so weak that they cannot govern themselves from one day to the next. They do not keep their prayer appointments with the Lord, or their spiritual vows, and if they take up Christian service their fellow workers despair of them because they never know if or when they will turn up, or whether they will remember the things they have undertaken to do. They may be strapping fellows, or energetic and strong-minded women, but their capacity for self-discipline, timekeeping, and fulfilling of promises is minimal, and this inevitably undermines loyalty to God, which is the essence of faith.

Self-discipline strengthens faith by the following route. Faith must be exercised against the pull of a fallen nature which constantly urges the believer to trust in himself, or to depend on some earthly crutch, or to prefer earthly things, or to despair under pressure. Strength is needed to reject the world, the flesh and the devil, and to live for the Lord, obey His commands, and trust His promises. But from where shall the believer obtain this strength to exercise faith? Firstly, of course, from the glorious truths of the Word that move him to loyalty to Christ. Secondly from the Spirit, in answer to prayer. But also, from the inner self-discipline developed in sanctification and everyday life. If this has become weak because the believer has capitulated to every desire and succumbed to every passing whim, he will be unable to fight the fight of faith.

We need to take ourselves in hand, deny ourselves unnecessary acquisitions, ration our entertainments and earthly pleasures, curb our time-wasting, and monitor our reliability for the Lord. By these measures our lives will know greater zeal and committedness, and strength to manage and control ourselves will be increased, so that faith also will become firmer and stronger. To summarise, even the duties of the Christian life buttress and strengthen faith.

3

Faith's Companion Virtues

'Giving all diligence, add to your faith virtue; and to virtue knowledge; and to knowledge temperance; and to temperance patience . . .' ***(2 Peter 1.5-6).***

WE LEARN MUCH about faith from looking at faith's 'conjunctive' texts, where faith is coupled with some other virtue or good act as in *Philippians 2.17*: 'Yea, and if I be offered upon the *sacrifice and service* of your faith, I joy, and rejoice with you all.' Paul frequently coupled various words together with faith to show its full scope and function. Faith is rather like a car engine which cannot be put to any use without the body of the car, and without a gearbox, wheels, petrol and a driver. Try to leave any of these items out, and the engine cannot be put to use. Similarly, faith can only thrive, function and increase when it is accompanied by the duties and virtues it activates. We cannot pick and choose these because all are vital to faith, and faith is vital to all. These duties and virtues are described in the challenging family of conjunctive or linkage texts.

Faith Linked with Sacrifice and Service

In *Philippians 2.17* (just quoted), we read of the sacrifice and service of faith. Living faith is always ready to make sacrifices, and if we refuse to make these we stunt our faith. It works in this way: if I am really persuaded and convinced about the Lord and His mission on earth (faith), then I feel very deeply that the only purpose of my being here is to serve Him and bring glory to His name. True faith cannot bear the idea of being useless and fruitless spiritually. With true faith I believe that if I yield myself to Him and serve Him for all I am worth, He will bless and use me, granting me instrumentality in His service. This faith does not count the cost or begrudge the time or money, and it never regrets yielding up energy and resources to the service of the Lord. Am I not particularly dedicated or available to the Lord? Do I hold back all my energy and resources for myself and for my own pleasure, comfort and ease? If so I cramp and impede the zeal and willingness of faith, and it shrivels and spoils.

Faith Linked with Love

In *1 Thessalonians 5.8* Paul makes another intriguing link, saying, 'But let us, who are of the day, be sober, putting on the breastplate of faith *and love*.' A breastplate is essential for defence, and here faith and love go hand in hand as the defence of the believer. The linking of faith and love shows that they must be exercised together. Our faith in God (that is – being convinced of His being and His saving kindness) joins hands with love for Him, meaning we will desire Him and His Word more than any earthly thing. This is the protective breastplate of the believer, and with these linked virtues we can withstand temptation and trial. We cannot deeply love God if we are not fully convinced of Him (faith), nor can we maintain deep faith in God if we do not love Him sincerely. Faith and love therefore need each other. If someone is content to be a cold, unenthusiastic believer with poor devotion, imagining he can still have strong faith, he fools himself, because faith cannot thrive without love. Similarly, if someone thinks he can love the Lord without diligently and daily exercising faith in His Word and ways he misleads himself, because without active faith, real love will be reduced to shallow sentiment.

Another aspect of faith and love is presented in *2 Thessalonians 1.3*: 'We are bound to thank God always for you, brethren, as it is meet, because that your faith groweth exceedingly, and the charity *[love]* of every one of you all toward each other aboundeth.' Here the apostle has in mind love between believers. We have noted in the previous chapter that active faith in God stimulates love between believers, and a lack of love for fellow believers stifles faith. When believers are unduly reserved and distant from each other, or when they have feuds and disregard each other, or when they avoid speaking to each other, or when gossip separates them, then faith is spoiled because Christ's command to His people to love one another is being flouted. In these circumstances only hypocritical faith exists. Faith strengthens love among Christian people, while refusal to love blights faith.

Faith Linked with Patience

Another 'linkage' text is found in *2 Thessalonians 1.4*, which reads: 'So that we ourselves glory in you in the churches of God for your *patience* and faith.' Here is a more obvious connection, but no less powerful for that. When faith is active it naturally leads to patience (literally, perseverance) in trials because we are convinced that God has a sovereign plan, that He really does intervene in our lives, that He knows our every state and condition, and that He will infallibly see us through. Possessing such a conviction must lead to and encourage patience. On the other hand, if we are not prepared to attempt to exercise patience, we will quickly undermine our faith. If we are habitually impatient, testy and short-fused, we contradict our beliefs, and injure our faith, because faith cannot be exercised in an atmosphere of impatience. The two support or hurt each other.

Faith Linked with Power

Yet another linkage text is to be seen in *2 Thessalonians 1.11*, where Paul says: 'Wherefore also we pray always for you, that our God would count you worthy of this calling, and fulfil all the good pleasure of his goodness, and the work of faith with *power*.' Faith and power, like faith and patience, are logically connected. If faith is exercised constantly in prayer and obedience to the Lord, then we shall experience the power of God in sanctification, witness, service, and the handling of trials. However, if we are not concerned to prove God's power and fail to pray for help there will be no blessing and consequently our faith will become disillusioned and diminished. Faith leads to our proving the Lord and, conversely, a desire to prove the Lord leads to faith being exercised and strengthened.

These conjunctive texts help us to see the context in which faith thrives, and to respect and follow after its closely associated values and duties.

4

The Causes of Peter's Little Faith

'And in the fourth watch of the night Jesus went unto them, walking on the sea . . . And Peter . . . said, Lord, if it be thou, bid me come unto thee on the water. And he said, Come' ***(Matthew 14.25, 28-29).***

THE ACCOUNT of Peter walking on the sea yields rich lessons on the subject of active faith, particularly as he possessed it at the outset and lost it during the course of the miracle. Peter asked for the invitation to walk on the water because he truly believed that the Lord could bring this about, and he was bold and eager to climb over the side of the vessel and go to Him. Realising that Christ possessed power to do amazing and remarkable things he exercised real faith, yet it did not last, and here lies a crucial lesson on faith. We are therefore looking at a disciple who exercised faith in obedience to Christ's word, experienced total vindication, and then suddenly collapsed into doubt, yielding to a spasm of unbelief. Like Peter, all converted people are sometimes 'unbelieving believers' mixing faith with doubt, showing how much of the old nature is still within. We have a new nature, thank God, but we also have residual sin and the old nature, one of its chief features being unbelief, always present and ready to express itself.

The key words in Matthew's account of Peter's walk are found in the rescue verse: 'And immediately Jesus stretched forth his hand, and caught him, and said unto him, O thou of little faith, wherefore didst thou doubt?' When Christ asks a question it is not because He needs to know the answer, for He knows it already, but for the benefit of the person to whom He speaks, and the readers of Scripture. The question 'Why did you doubt?' is a plea to Peter to think about the cause of his faith's failure, and to learn from it.

Why did Peter doubt? The usual answer is that he took his eyes off the Lord, and while this may be true, the text does not specifically say so. It tells us that he observed the wind and the waves, and these swept away his faith. It was not by literally looking at the Lord that Peter would be sustained above the waves, but by remembering that Christ Who possessed divine power had commanded him to come.

But how did Peter's forgetfulness of Christ's command and power come about? His faith failed when he became overawed by his circumstances. This was the point when he stopped reasoning as a believer, the waves driving out of his mind the evidence of Christ's power he had seen while on shore. Fear caused him to forget that it was the Lord Who had commanded him to walk on the water, and blotted out his awareness that the person standing so near to him on the water was the infallible Lord of Glory. Fear even eradicated from his mind his astonishing achievement of having already walked a number of paces on the surface of the waves. All powerful supports to his faith were forgotten in an instant, his last remaining vestige of faith crying out, 'Lord, save me!'

It is strange that Peter had enough faith in the Lord to venture on to the water, but not to believe that the Lord would sustain him. Then, as soon as he began to sink, he manifested faith once again, calling on Christ to rescue him. We observe in Peter a mixture of belief and unbelief, faith and mistrust, and how like him we are, feeling certain that God can help us, save us, and take us to glory, but frequently lacking the faith to believe that He can see us through our present circumstances. Why should it be harder to have faith for sustaining blessing than for commencing it? Doubt is so subtle, and if we do nothing to evict it we will eventually suffer a rebuke from the Lord as Peter did.

The Lord's challenge to Peter was – 'Why did you doubt?' The passage provides five answers to this question, all of which are relevant to our moments of doubting today.

1. Doubts in a New Environment

Peter was accustomed to being in a boat, but as soon as he stepped outside that supportive, protective vessel his faith failed to hold up, and this is so often why faith fails. As soon as the journey of faith takes us out of our 'element' we start to feel insecure and the real testing begins. A believer may enter a new stage in life, study or career, moving into an uncharted future, and so stepping out of the familiar boat into an area where faith has never before been exercised. Will it hold up or cease to operate? A great shock or a trial never faced before may also 'surprise' our faith and leave us floundering and reacting in the same way as unbelievers. Every day, therefore, we should pray along the lines of the Lord's Prayer, 'Lead us not into temptation' – a petition that faith will not be caught out by new situations. Even among pastors and seminary teachers new surroundings and new chapters in life can overpower faith and spiritual obedience, turning us into 'unbelieving believers'. Watch out for new environments.

2. Failure to Nourish Faith

Immediately before the incident on the sea the disciples had been involved in the feeding of the five thousand, a spectacular miracle. One might expect that the memory of this would still have been deeply impressed on Peter's mind when he walked on the water, but apparently his faith had not been nourished and stimulated by reflecting on the event. Perhaps if he and the other disciples had sat in their storm-tossed vessel remembering how thousands had been fed, their sense of wonder and their faith would still have been strong when the Lord came to them walking on the water. We frequently go wrong even after having received some distinctive evidence of God's goodness by talking about everything except the wonderful power of God. We fail to commit such blessings to memory for future encouragement, allowing a few difficulties and heartaches to blow the blessing away.

It is often similar with the hearing of ministry. How many believers, after hearing a sermon which has lifted them up, promptly go home and yield their mind and attention to something completely secular or unspiritual, chatting about anything other than the things of God? The impact and benefit of the sermon is swiftly washed out of the mind, leaving them less equipped to face Satan's attacks on their faith. Peter spent a relatively short time in the storm, but when his faith was tested it became obvious that it had not been fed and strengthened in readiness.

One of the main causes of doubting is that believers get out of practice at exercising faith, asking for little and receiving little from God. This may be due to coldness of heart or a failure of personal discipline. Let us suppose that a Sunday School teacher's heart has grown so cold that he becomes unconcerned what happens to his children. He teaches the Truth but no longer agonises much over whether they take it in and whether it saves them. Such a teacher is unlikely to plead for their souls, and unlikely, consequently, to be blessed with instrumentality. Lacking the blessing that comes from answered prayer, whatever remnant of faith he has left will eventually disappear because he receives no heart-warming evidence to encourage it. Faith not exercised will be faith reduced. The heart must be kept in sympathy with the cause of Christ and the winning of souls at all cost, by reflecting on the great blessings that He gives, and returning thanks. Erosion of faith by indiscipline and laziness, by not getting down to daily, trusting prayer and intercession, is sadly common in a culture so full of distractions.

3. Failure to Respect Christ's Command and Power

In the case of Peter, we have observed that he momentarily forgot that Christ had commanded him to walk on the water, giving him an express commission. If only he had remembered that he was acting under the orders of God he would have reasoned that if the Lord had told him to do it, it must be the right thing to do, and that God must intend to sustain him. Christ's commands are also promises.

We noted earlier in this book that some Christians misunderstand faith, thinking it is a matter of mustering the will-power to believe that something will definitely happen. Faith, however, is not a belief that God will do anything we want, as long as we believe hard enough, but that God has the power to do anything that *He* decides to do. Let us imagine that Peter had made up his own mind to walk on the water because he thought it was a good idea, and accordingly he exercised faith that Christ would look after him, and set off. The result, probably, would have been that he immediately sank. However, Peter knew better than that, and asked Christ to call him, by which he would know that this exploit would be the Saviour's will.

There are many cases of needed blessing where we already know the will of God, because He has already revealed it in His Word, and in these cases we may proceed in faith certain that God will bless us. For example, God has commanded sinners to repent and believe the Gospel, and it is therefore safe to do so. As we sincerely yield to Him we can be certain that He will respond to us, because we are doing what He has commanded and invited us to do.

Christ commands us to feed on His Word daily, to pray to Him regularly, to hear His Word, to serve Him, to witness for Him and to maintain spiritual priorities. He also commands us to be scrupulously honest in all things, and to keep apart from false doctrine. If some stress or difficulty arises on account of any of His commands, we dare not abandon them in order to resolve our difficulties. We must believe that if we cry out to Him in faith, He will always sustain us to obey His commands. We therefore say, if Christ commands us in His Word to adopt a certain lifestyle for His name's sake, or to carry out any difficult task, we will do it, because His command not only compels us, but also reassures us of His intention to sustain us. His commands are our great assurance.

There are numerous desired blessings which are not absolutely promised to us in the Word, such as healing, or greater wealth, or marriage, or pastoral calling, and in these cases we should not presume they will be ours, or 'claim' them from God, as unbiblical teachers today urge us to do. For such things we may wish to pray, but always with submission to God's supreme and infinitely wise will.

It is true that Peter had the idea of walking on the sea in the first place, but Christ endorsed it and expressly commanded him to walk, and so his faith rested on the expressed will of Christ and in His mighty power. We also note that Peter was initially successful in walking on the water, and while we do not know how many steps he took, some old writers think he went quite a way as he was within arm's length of the Saviour when he began to sink. The significant point about Peter's early success is that he would have experienced a tremendous surge of elation, receiving sure proof of the power and authority of Christ. If only he had treasured this in his mind, giving heartfelt thanks to the Lord, surely he would have been protected from the alarms of the boisterous wind! The application for us is that we should never take for granted any blessing from God, leaving it unremembered and unresponded to with praise. Such blessings are the supports of future faith.

4. Forgetfulness of Christ's Love

Another cause of doubt involved in Peter's case is that he lost his realisation of Christ's close interest in him. He momentarily lost sight of the fact that the Lord of the waves, Who successfully walked on the water Himself, was within touching distance of him. Astonishing though this may seem, fear overpowered his faith even when the Lord was so near. His moment of panic could only come about because he lost his awareness of Christ's immeasurable affection for him, and His everlasting interest in his progress and concerns. Alongside this Peter seems to have forgotten that Christ is always faithful, and His perfectly faithful heart can never discard those whom He has made His own. Once again it could be said that Peter's loss of faith arose from his forgetfulness.

The lesson here is that unless we make the effort to keep in mind the Lord's interest in us, and also His faithful character, our faith may fail even when we are enjoying close communion with Him. It is always vital to reflect on the loving kindness of Christ and to maintain praise and thankfulness, not only because it is His due, but also because our own faith is nourished and sustained. Sometimes believers make little attempt to reflect on the love of Christ, and so do not keep their gratitude and certainty bright and alive. There is little thankfulness in their hearts and no praise in their life, God's love being as much taken for granted as the air they breathe, and faith consequently withers in their hearts.

5. Self-reliance, Not Dependence

Doubting may also be defined as a state of mind that arises when we begin to plan our lives and decide how to respond to circumstances as though there were no God in Heaven and everything depended upon us. This particular form of doubt is just as likely to afflict ministers as any other believer, because no one is immune. Self-reliance is not an obvious fault of Peter's in the incident of walking on the sea, but it is implied by his characteristic forwardness, being the only disciple to think of doing such a thing. He was frequently the first to volunteer, the first to speak, and the first to assert his loyalty even to death. In his mind there was no reason why he could not succeed (with the Lord's help), and not the slightest fear that his faith might not be strong enough. Alongside his faith, and perhaps larger than his faith, lurked self-reliance, and this would contribute to his failure.

The person who is most endowed with planning and organising ability may well be the person most prone to self-reliance, but any strong gift may produce it. The practice of sincerely committing everything to the Lord in prayer is vital to the maintaining of faith. Then when the 'impossible' situation arises, allowed by the Lord to test, demonstrate and increase our faith, we will prove Him gloriously.

As believers we are here to trust the Lord and to prove His sustaining and guiding power. He is the superintendent and director of our affairs, and the God Who sees us through them to His honour and glory. We plunge into doubt and unbelief, often without recognising it, whenever we proceed to solve our problems as though we were strong enough of ourselves, needing only *some* help from the Lord – the folly of self-reliance.

We turn next in this book to the major testing of faith that comes through temptations to doubt, whether the promises of God, our own salvation or the doctrines of the faith. These fiery darts of the devil must be expected, recognised, and countered with the shield of faith, for if faith does not defend itself it will quickly become ineffective.

Dealing with Doubts

– PART TWO –

5

Causes and Cure of Doubts

'Finally, my brethren, be strong in the Lord, and in the power of his might. Put on the whole armour of God, that ye may be able to stand against the wiles of the devil' ***(Ephesians 6.10-11).***

ALL BELIEVERS ARE assailed by doubts in some shape or form, and though some say that they are not greatly troubled in this way, the reality is they do not recognise doubts which come in subtle disguises. When Paul speaks of Satan's *wiles* he uses a word which refers to the crafty methods of an enemy who seldom attacks in broad daylight, hurling obvious doubts, but mostly by insinuating into the mind unnoticed doubts. Satan rings no alarm bells and sounds no sirens. He seeks to bring believers into a condition of doubting very quietly, so that they do not realise what is happening to them. It is his *wiles,* his cunning manoeuvres, we should be concerned about. From Satan's point of view *conscious* doubts are inferior to unconscious ones because they stir up a believer's spiritual concern, jarring his soul and driving him to the

Lord in prayer. By conscious doubts the devil may certainly cause temporary damage to joy and peace, but by unconscious ones, such as a somewhat cynical attitude to the Christian lifestyle, he may cripple faith for a long time.

Watchfulness is Vital

Some Christians expose themselves to doubts because they do not expect to be troubled by them. Some think that doubts recede as believers grow in faith, but we can never have too much faith for the devil to lose interest in us. The more we prove the Lord and grow in grace and instrumentality, the more our evil enemy will want to make fools of us and ruin our testimony. We must therefore expect his wiles and be ready for them.

A believer who is unconsciously cynical will be characterised by complacency and inactivity, with a lack of warmth, fervour and commitment to the Lord. Satan's crowning achievement is for such a person to have no *obvious* and troubling doubts or assurance problems. We know that the devil works to fairly regular patterns in the operating of his wiles because Paul is able to say, 'we are not ignorant of his devices.' Like a commander in warfare Satan has a range of strategies and procedures, selecting whichever is appropriate for the individual believer. He is methodical also in the way in which he tailors his attacks to take advantage of our weaknesses and areas of neglect, so that if we are currently omitting some spiritual duty, or permitting ourselves certain sins, the devil will design an assault which will take full advantage of these backslidings. He knows our most frequent sins, observes all those luxuries which our hearts have become fond of, and remembers the temptations which have succeeded in bringing us down before. In the light of all these things he plots precisely how and when he will make shipwreck of our spiritual lives. In *Ephesians 6.16* the apostle exhorts in these words: 'Above all, taking the shield of faith, wherewith ye shall be able to quench all the fiery darts of the wicked.' Though we received new hearts and spiritual life at conversion, we are still in the body, and lingering fleshly inclinations remain, known as residual sin. Chief among the old crimes of our unconverted days was that of doubting God, and a residue of this still lurks in the dark recesses of every saved heart, ready to be activated by Satan's darts of doubts. In every believer a fragment of unbelieving Pharisee waits for its opportunity to break out and vent cynical murmurings. These doubts, as we have said, generally come quietly and unobtrusively, although sometimes they may strike with a mighty blow and seem for a moment almost impossible to surmount.

I remember a Christian couple who were so disturbed by doubts that they lost all hope of recovering spiritual happiness, and worship and prayer became meaningless and hypocritical for them. The trial began when one of them became anxious about a particular point of doctrine, leading them to talk and worry about this matter long into the night hours. Eventually the doubts of one became the doubts of both, the issue being tortuously and repeatedly examined until they began to suffer a form of revulsion not unusual in severe 'doubting' trials. They developed near contempt for the fellow believers in their fellowship, looking around and thinking, 'Oh, these superficial people who find it so easy to believe anything they are told.'

These two almost lost their faith entirely, yet at the same time managed to think that they were the most mature and intelligent believers because they alone had experienced such deep spiritual reservations. It is a tragic situation when the devil succeeds in the double aim of planting doubts and pride at the same time. Any concern over a point of doctrine should always be thought out in the context of heartfelt, expressed affirmation of the truths that are so clear and dear to us.

1. Doubting of Personal Salvation

All believers may be tempted at some time to *doubt their own salvation*, for Satan is bound to try taking away our joy and peace in believing. At such times the faith itself is not doubted, but serious doubts are fired into the mind about the individual's personal standing in the faith.

2. Doubting the Promises

Even more commonly believers are tempted to doubt *the Lord's promises to protect and guide them.* This is a major form of unconscious doubt which arises when a Christian is suddenly confronted by a disturbing situation, and is inclined to react in panic and self-pity as though there were no Saviour, no Guide, no Comforter, and no Answerer of prayer. A voice within, but one which is not consciously heard, seems to say, 'God cannot protect me in this!' and the believer behaves in accordance with that voice. We should never allow ourselves to forget the 'exceeding greatness of his power to us-ward who believe', nor let the 'flesh' speak first, complaining and murmuring as soon as problems occur. We should never permit our minds to be filled with discontent and morbid reflections, nor blame our friends, fellow Christians or anyone else for our difficulties. Self-pity is one of the most common forms of doubting, yet many a victim would never recognise it as such.

3. Doubting Service for God

A dedicated, serving believer may at some time be tempted to doubt the *usefulness and effectiveness of the work of God*, especially when tired, so that the mind is filled with despondency and pessimism. We know how quickly such feelings undermine and sabotage our labours, and so preachers, evangelists, Sunday School teachers, district visitors and witnessing Christians all need to keep in mind the commanding words of the great commission, because from them we learn that labour for the Lord is Christ's purpose for us, and its usefulness cannot therefore be questioned. In addition we have the strong assurances of fruit in famous texts of promise, among the most memorable being *1 Corinthians 15.58*: 'Therefore, my beloved brethren, be ye stedfast, unmoveable, always abounding in the work of the Lord, forasmuch as ye know that your labour is not in vain in the Lord.'

Also precious are *1 Corinthians 3.8, Galatians 6.9, Psalm 126.5-6, Isaiah 40.21-31,* and *Isaiah 41.10, 13-15.* The reassuring words of Christ recorded in *John 15.16* certainly refer to the fruit of holiness, but equally they promise the fruit of conversion: 'Ye have not chosen me, but I have chosen you, and ordained you, that ye should go and bring forth fruit, and that your fruit should remain: that whatsoever ye shall ask of the Father in my name, he may give it you.' These verses and many others are intended to answer Satan's insinuations about the value of a Christian's witness, and if these are treasured and affirmed regularly, such temptations to doubt are not able to take root.

4. Doubting Joy of Communion

Another very common form of doubt is the temptation to doubt the *enjoyability of communion with the Lord.* Just when it is time for personal devotions, though the believer may have looked forward to this moment, prayer suddenly seems like a gloomy shadow, an irksome and burdensome duty. In a moment of intense demonic suggestion, almost anything else seems more interesting and important – even the worst household chore. Secular matters seem brighter and better and more rewarding than time with the Lord.

It does not even seem to help the believer to remember that the last time this form of doubt was experienced its futile nature was soon exposed, because once he began to pray his heart was immediately warmed and cheered and the profound enjoyability of personal prayer was proved once again. This problem is not normally classified as a temptation to doubt, but it is, and it must be recognised and resisted as such.

5. Doubting the Doctrines

Temptations to doubt *the faith* are more likely in the earliest days of Christian experience, but then it would seem that Satan lays this type of temptation aside for a while to concentrate on some of the other forms of doubt we have referred to. When he returns with doubts of the faith, he typically questions some particular aspect of Christian Truth. He may plan these temptations to coincide with stages of life marking periods of change and adaptation. Advice for countering and even preventing doubting of the faith follows later in this chapter.

6. Doubting the Standards

An extremely widespread kind of temptation to doubt focuses on *the standards* and blueprints given by God for the lifestyle of believers and the conduct of churches. The question arises in evangelical circles – What is normative or authoritative for today in the Bible? We realise well enough that some of the practices of the early church are to be seen in their cultural context, such as the injunction to greet one another with a holy kiss, such practices not necessarily being binding on Christians today, except in principle. We know that there is often a different way of expressing something in another culture and age, so today we would regard the handshake as a reasonable equivalent to the kiss. But many teachers today want to extend that liberty of interpretation to just about everything in the Scriptures if they can, and so they surround numerous plain commands of the Bible which *are* binding with 'cultural' speculation and doubt.

In effect, Satan still whispers to believers, 'Yea, hath God said?' Has God really said His people should avoid this or that? Has God really forbidden friendship with the world, worldly lifestyles, mingling with false teachers, ecumenical evangelism, and so forth? Does He really insist that women should not preach? A constant barrage of doubting temptations takes the form of questions about the standards which God requires of us. Are they relevant for today, or may we doubt and flout these ancient principles? The author has tried to set out the way in which we may distinguish culture-bound matters from binding matters in his book, *Not Like Any Other Book*, and would invite concerned readers to consult this.*

An Antidote to Doubting

The *shield of faith (Ephesians 6.16)* is our most important preventive measure against temptations to doubt, the word *faith* indicating a state of being entirely persuaded and convinced that something is true. It is helpful to distinguish between *biblical* faith, and the kind of faith so often exercised by Roman Catholics, which is called *implicit* faith. Implicit faith means that the 'faithful' person does not have to be personally convinced about any particular doctrine or practice, but unquestioningly accepts the whole 'package' on the authority of the Church. He does not have to understand the details of his religion, and may have many potential doubts, but whatever his Church believes he is content to accept unreservedly.

Biblical faith, by contrast, means being fully convinced about all the saving and central doctrines of God's Word for oneself. A truly converted person anointed by the Spirit at conversion becomes wholly *persuaded* in heart and mind of the person and work of Christ and the inspiration and infallibility of the Bible. But here is the danger. It is possible for a true convert who has been convinced about the fundamentals of the faith to lapse into *implicit* faith for all other doctrines. Such a person has true faith for the basic doctrines of personal salvation, but merely accepts everything else 'on trust', saying, 'My church and pastor teach it from the Bible therefore it must be true and I believe it.' Obviously, this is not a safe way to believe. Biblical faith requires earnest personal conviction, in which the teaching is fully grasped, embraced and enjoyed. This is how faith is defined in *Hebrews 11* where we are told that the Old Testament heroes of faith saw the promises of God from afar 'and were

---

* *Not Like Any Other Book, Interpreting the Bible,* Peter Masters, Wakeman Trust, London, 2004; ISBN 1 870855 43 4.

persuaded of them, and embraced them'. If, after conversion, we accept further doctrinal teaching lightly, believing it only because our church teaches it and not because it has become clear and precious to us, then we will be extremely vulnerable to the attacks of Satan. It is these vaguely acknowledged doctrines which he will first tempt us to doubt, plunging us into painful confusion, and then he will be able to challenge fundamentals.

The great preventive measure is for us to be earnest students of all the faith. This does not mean we become furrowed-browed, unteachable cynics, but we must drink deeply of the truth we hear, taking the 'sword of the Spirit, which is the word of God' and praying for genuine understanding and appreciation of all the doctrines. If we are diligent students of doctrine, then the gracious Holy Spirit will help us to value all that we discern and the enemy will have the greatest difficulty in sweeping us from our moorings. Once we have been so impressed by a truth that we stand in awe of it and wonder at its marvellous depths, then as far as that truth is concerned, we shall be strongly fortified against the fiery darts of doubt.

The *shield of faith* is a state of mind reached when we are convinced and persuaded about biblical truths and trust them to be true. The believer draws his shield from the armoury of thought and devotion, a fact which shows the importance of personal devotions. These should be more than a quick reading and a prayer, and must be accompanied by eager study of the faith, even taking notes in teaching services, and seeking advice and direction whenever we become aware of any deficiency in our grasp of something. Every believer, however greatly or little educated, may by grace comprehend and enjoy the whole faith, and so possess the great shield of firm conviction and trust which blocks the fiery darts of doubt.

Dealing with Great Intellectual Difficulties

We return to *direct* temptations to doubt, and particularly to the tactic of the devil when he takes one or two difficult points of doctrine and questions them, plunging us into a state of confusion and unease. His aim is to cast a shadow of uncertainty over our whole trust in the Lord. He may strike when we are climbing some high mountain of Truth, investigating the rarefied atmosphere of sovereign grace mysteries perhaps, of God's decree, of election, or some other sublime theme. We may, for example, be trying to understand how the impenitent, whose wills are bound by sin, can be held responsible for their unbelief, or to what extent God has determined reprobation and hardened the hearts of the lost. Whatever the topic, at some stage the scornful, cynical questions of Satan may begin to be inserted into the stream of our thinking, questions intended to harass and trouble the mind and to cast a slur on the love and fairness of God.

We may panic in our thinking like birds caught in a snare, struggling until our minds become exhausted and the behaviour of our God seems arbitrary and unreasonable. By now the darts of doubt are becoming embedded in our minds and our trust and reverence are seriously undermined. Does God not care that countless people must be forfeited to eternal punishment so that His sovereignty and His glorious justice may be vindicated? Once our thoughts take this route, more and more doubts will occur until the whole fabric of our faith may be shaken and we lose our joy and assurance.

We will have succumbed to 'tunnel vision' syndrome, in which Satan succeeds in pressing us in such a way that we stare constantly at one difficulty until everything becomes distorted and unnatural to us. If we ever find ourselves floundering in a sea of confusion because of a morbid preoccupation with one point of the law which we cannot understand we should take up the shield of faith.

Wielding the *shield of faith* means putting aside for the moment the problem issues, to review and affirm the things we are sure about. Are we not completely convinced and persuaded that this is a rebellious world, and that sin is rampant in it? Are we not convinced about human depravity through the Fall? Are we not persuaded that mankind is cut off from a God Who is holy, gracious and merciful? Are we not certain of the unique character and integrity of the Bible? Are we not convinced that the only hope for our souls is that Christ came to suffer and die on Calvary? Have we not proved the reality of conversion, that this is a real and a transforming experience? Has not our faith been fully vindicated both in its explanation of our world and through our personal experience of God's mighty love and power? And have we not proved the power of prayer?

As we review our certainties and blessings we will realise with alarm how much the devil has already deceived us, causing us to lose sight of things we have proved. It is almost as though we have agreed to his terms in this encounter, namely, that our faith will stand or fall on the outcome of a single difficulty. God *has* done wonderful things for us in showing us the depravity of this world and of our own hearts. He has given us His Word and proved Himself to us in a thousand ways, and we must see difficult questions in this context. In the case of the examples mentioned earlier, the formulation of our thinking must always be that whatever God does is perfect and fair and kind. Only when these great facts are sincerely affirmed can we approach deep problems correctly.

This is not a technique which will turn us into obscurantists. It is not suggested that we jettison our problems of faith as though they do not exist, but we must set them *in perspective*, in the light of all those truths which are certain and true to us. Holding the *shield of faith* we say, 'I know that the Lord is certain, the Bible is certain, conversion is certain, my faith is certain, but I have come across a problem here and it is troubling me. I wish I could solve this difficulty; I would like some light on the matter. But I will not permit my inquiry to insult my glorious God, or detract from any of His eternal attributes.'

Imagine a large military force sitting still and allowing one or two guerrillas to work their way through the ranks slaughtering everyone. Any part of that large force could cut them down in a moment, but strong, heavily-armed men sit passively while their entire battalion is eliminated. We must not let anything like this happen in our spiritual lives, allowing the many powerful truths which we have already proved to be slaughtered by individual doubts.

In dealing with a burning dart of doubt it often helps to adopt the inspired approach of Isaiah recorded in the prophet's great 'comfort' chapters. As he sought to build up once again the faith of the spiritual remnant within Israel he invited them to imagine what it would be like if they were idolaters, without God and without hope. He challenged the spiritual and intellectual status of the pagan world, saying, 'Produce your cause, saith the Lord; bring forth your strong reasons, saith the King of Jacob. Let them bring them forth, and shew us what shall happen: let them shew the former things, what they be . . . or declare us things for to come' *(Isaiah 41.21-22).*

Instead of being cast down by the devil's doubting insinuations, we should adopt a similar approach and put our doubts on the run. We should view the unconverted, unbelieving world (yet never without sympathy and compassion) and ask ourselves if we really want to go back to their condition. Do we wish to be back on the world's side, without light and hope, and devoid of understanding of spiritual things and God's sovereign plans and purposes? Would we like to lose our new heart, new nature, and spiritual awareness of the presence of the Lord? Would we like to be, once again, members of the enslaved army of lost people under the dominion of the prince of the power of the air? Would we like to be people who cannot understand why the world is like it is, and are unaware of things that must surely come to pass?

To hold up the *shield of faith* is to review our certain convictions, and then to peep round it and remind ourselves of the plight of the lost, so that we feel ashamed and gain a renewed appreciation of all our blessings. But having done this, we must still return to the particular problem which has thrown us into anxiety and confusion, and this is where the apostle's other exhortation guides us, 'Finally, my brethren, be strong in the Lord.' When thinking through difficult issues we cannot be *strong* (literally – made able) from our own mental resources for we are grappling with high and mysterious themes which go beyond the limit of human understanding. We are also affected by our fleshly nature which makes it hard to consider these themes from God's point of view. Our intellects are corrupted by the programming of our rebellious race, and our ideas about what is fair and just are prejudiced and earthly.

Let us then root our thinking in the Lord, and begin with His certain attributes. There is no theological conundrum which should not bow first to the character and heart of God. We are called to make all our judgements on the basis of God's revelation of Himself in His Word, and supremely in the person of the Lord Jesus Christ our Saviour. Am I tempted to think that a doctrine makes God seem unfair, arbitrary, impatient, unreasonable or unkind? Then I must look at my Lord. Do I see my Saviour reflecting any of these traits? Of course not, for I see Him healing men and women, suffering their spite and unbelief, then dying in inexpressible agony as the Friend of sinners. I see His heart full of compassion, even for His enemies. I see Him weeping over the city and lamenting for the daughters of Jerusalem. I hear His pleading words, and I realise afresh the unfathomable, tender love of Christ toward lost mankind.

I see all the attributes of God displayed in the Word, and I say to myself, 'Whatever doubts may arise in my mind, I know that the Almighty God, my Father, my Saviour, and the gracious Holy Spirit, are infinitely wonderful, pure and just, and could and would never do anything unfair, unreasonable, monstrous or unkind.' We must start here, with the things we know, grounding all our thinking in the Lord. Only here are we safe from being tossed about on the vain sea of doubt and speculation. Only here shall we gain a better understanding of any difficult point which may have previously exhausted our minds, restricted our power of reason, enveloped us in anxiety, and blinded us from the sight and comfort of all the wonderful things we have already proved to be true.

However, what if this procedure helps deliver us from hurtful doubts but leads us no nearer to solving our intellectual difficulty? What if some rarefied item of Truth still causes disquiet? Let us remember that growth in spiritual understanding is a gradual matter. Things we do not fully grasp now, we will understand in the future. We are given very many *certainties* so that we may exercise *loving trust* in any matters yet to be understood. This is not *implicit* faith because we are aiming at achieving a better understanding of the perplexing doctrine. Faith rests on the certainties, and trusts God to unfold the hidden heights and depths, perhaps in the months ahead, and perhaps for some matters in the glory to come. Faith keeps her hold on the great things which God has already revealed, seeking progress, but not demanding all at once. Faith is patient, not frustrated, saying with the psalmist –

> **'Lord, my heart is not haughty, nor mine eyes lofty: neither do I exercise myself in great matters, or in things too high for me. Surely I have behaved and quieted myself, as a child that is weaned of his mother: my soul is even as a weaned child. Let Israel hope in the Lord from henceforth and for ever' *(Psalm 131).***

George Rawson wrote in the spirit of that psalm when he penned the following lines:

My Father, it is good for me
To trust and not to trace;
And wait with deep humility
For Thy revealing grace.

Lord, when Thy way is in the sea,
And strange to mortal sense,
I see Thee in the mystery,
And trust Thy providence.

I cannot grasp the secret things
In this my dark abode;
I may not reach with earthly wings
The heights and depths of God.

So, faith and patience! wait awhile,
Not doubting, not in fear;
For soon in Heaven my Father's smile
Shall render all things clear.

Then Thou shalt end time's short eclipse,
Its dim uncertain night;
Bring in the grand apocalypse,
Reveal the perfect light.

Coping with Trials

– PART THREE –

6

The Shipwreck of Paul and the Trials of Believers

'And falling into a place where two seas met, they ran the ship aground; and the forepart struck fast . . . but the hinder part was broken with the violence of the waves' *(Acts 27.41)*.

IN ACTS 27 we are given the extraordinary account of the shipwreck suffered by Paul while heading under military escort to Rome. Luke's record is surely superb, supplying an amazing amount of detail. There is always special significance in a long biblical narrative, and this one provides considerable information and counsel concerning the kind of trials which believers will encounter during their journey through life.

Although the true author of the chapter is, of course, the Holy Spirit, the narrative reflects the human style of Luke the beloved physician, and his remarkable powers of observation. We see that he knew his geography, and, though a landlubber, was fully conversant with seafaring terms. The incidental challenge of Luke's narrative lies in his evident capacity to notice unusual things and store them in his mind, and we could well study his record simply as an example of great Christian conversation. There is no pointless element, no dull information, no shallow hero-worship (not even of the great apostle), no exaggeration, and nothing carnal. Without falling to any of these defects Luke has produced a narrative full of drama, information and surprise.

However, the chief value of this record is the light that it throws on the trials through which believers may sail, and how these should be responded to. Our tendency is to lose sight of the inevitability of trials, and to react badly to them when they come. Paul was forewarned by the Lord that this particular voyage would bring trouble, and this came with the 'tempestuous wind' or *Hurricane Euroclydon* which ultimately wrecked the vessel. The first observation to make is that the apostle was not exempted from this terrifying experience. Do we sometimes imagine that because we are Christians we should never be put through circumstances or situations which hurt or terrify us? At times we may have to go through some very alarming experiences.

Luke records how the vessel was caught helplessly in the storm, unable to tack, and driven pitilessly in the direction of the wind. So anxious were the crew about the survival of the craft that they sent courageous men over the side to place ropes or chains under and round the hull to gird it tightly together, Luke providing the classic description of 'frapping' a ship. Even this was not enough, for as the battering continued and the vessel threatened to sink, they jettisoned the precious cargo.

Consider the extreme nature of this shipwreck, and note particularly how the meticulous Luke changes his pronouns at one point in the narrative to emphasise the unfolding catastrophe. He writes: 'And *we* being exceedingly tossed with a tempest, the next day *they* [the crew that is] lightened the ship; and the third day *we* [now with all the passengers helping] cast out with our own hands the tackling of the ship' *(Acts 27.18-19).* The situation became too much for the crew to handle, especially when the tackling had to be jettisoned, including the great main yard of the ship, that massive timber spar from which they hung the principal sail. We remember that this was a vessel of considerable size for the times, holding 276 people and much freight. This huge main yard had either crashed down, causing havoc as it rolled about on the deck, or it was about to fall. All sails had been torn to shreds and now whiplashed backwards and forwards with the tackling as the ship was hurled about. The situation was so dangerous that the vital yard-arm must somehow be bundled overboard.

James Smith in his nineteenth-century classic thesis, *The Voyage and Shipwreck of St Paul,* pictures the entire crew and passenger body lined up along the huge, threshing yard, to force the giant timber over the side, although from this point any possibility of survival became remote. As for Paul and Luke, their ministry was surely at an end, showing that even apostles and preachers may suffer seemingly terminal trials. As the days passed amidst unabating fury, the slenderest hope gave way to despair, Luke recalling: 'When neither sun nor stars in many days appeared, and no small tempest lay on us, all hope that we should be saved was then taken away.' Christians may be led through experiences so distressing that no hope is to be seen anywhere. We are not, therefore, to be surprised and broken in trials, as if such circumstances should never come upon believers.

Luke also tells us that they did not eat for most of the ordeal, clearly because the ship was heaving so much, and also because murderous waves swept across the deck so constantly that nothing could have been prepared. Believers may find themselves in a trial so great that they are deprived for a time of the most basic necessities and comforts of physical or spiritual life. About this time the Lord communicated to Paul reassuring words, just as He does to all believers at the height of a trial, in our case through His Word. Paul was moved to utter one of the most powerful faith-strengthening sentiments in the Bible, and one we should remember often – 'God, whose I am, and whom I serve'. Could we ever be deserted by our eternal, omnipotent, heavenly Master?

Consider Luke's magnificent handling of language as he conveys the grim situation toward the end: 'Then fearing lest we should have fallen upon rocks, they cast four anchors out of the stern, and wished for the day.' Christians may be called, in exceptional circumstances, to go through situations in which they can do nothing whatsoever to relieve the situation, except to pray. The beloved physician also describes how, as the vessel finally approached land, the passengers suffered an attempt by crew members to escape, abandoning them to shipwreck on the rocks. Christians are not exempt from being deserted by those from whom they should receive help and loyalty.

The last moments of the trial, the final destruction of the ship, brought a climax of terror when crew and passengers alike had to risk death by driving the vessel in the direction of a rocky creek and running it aground. 'They committed themselves unto the sea,' says Luke, for they could not accurately steer. We may imagine the uncertainty as the waves crashed about them and their shattered vessel twisted and heaved with only a lethal outline of rocks in view. The trust of Paul and Luke must now be entirely in the overruling hand of Almighty God. Soon the bow of the ship rammed sickeningly aground and the stern began to disintegrate under the pounding of the seas. The smashing and grinding of timbers and the drenching breakers shouted death and disaster as crew and passengers huddled in the bow, and even now the soldiers wanted to execute the prisoners. The only way of escape was to struggle to the shore on broken timbers, few people in those days knowing how to swim.

Who can deny, after reading this long shipwreck account, that God's choicest messengers are not spared the shocks and pains of very great hardships? The dust-jackets of many Christian books today give the impression that believers ought never to suffer such trials. Their authors tell us how we may walk with the Lord in such a way that we will never encounter serious problems, privations or sicknesses, or at least none which may not be easily resolved. They imagine that Christians are meant to be happy, healthy and victorious throughout their lives. Fortunately there are still many Christians who do not believe such nonsense, but even these may react to trials very poorly, recoiling with dismay and perhaps with a stream of complaints, or even with ill-tempered conduct. Some believers are not nice people when they are in trouble.

The question must be asked – Why exactly did Paul, Luke and their companions suffer this harrowing shipwreck experience? Were they guilty of sin? Was the shipwreck a chastisement or warning from the Lord? Such explanations should be dismissed promptly because there is not a word to support them in the entire narrative. The truth is that the Lord means His people to go through times of trouble for their sanctification and training, as well as (sometimes) for chastisement. One rather obvious purpose is the development of faith. How can faith be deepened and strengthened without trials and difficulties? It is largely by such experiences that we grow in dependence upon the Lord, learning to pray with true dependence, discovering His goodness, proving His faithfulness to His promises, and appreciating the greatness of His power toward His people.

However, there are other reasons why we must go through trials and tribulations, because Christians are meant to be a living demonstration to unbelievers. We are supposed to show to those around us that we really do have the help of God, and are genuinely in touch with Him; and how could we give a truly convincing demonstration of this without troubles? Unbelievers are not impressed merely by our claims, but they need to see how we behave in response to our difficulties. Our reactions to these will either establish or undermine our words. When we are at work or at college and things begin to happen which could wound or inflame us, how will we react? As our colleagues look on, what will they see – an unseemly tantrum or a peevish, unpleasant spirit? Will they see a demonstration of pride or selfishness or hostility? Will they witness the reaction of a person who has no depth of character and no help available from God? Unbelievers watch believers very carefully.

Suppose that we have to suffer an alarming or prolonged trial such as a serious illness or some heavy loss such as redundancy. How will we handle it? Trials provide a demonstration to the world around us of our true contact with the Lord, and to handle them well is a far more powerful testimony than words alone. Puritan John Trapp said: 'Present doings must not shame former sayings.'

Yet another purpose of trials is to wean us, as believers, from dependency upon or over-enjoyment of this world. The centurion in charge of Paul's escort was a cultured man who looked favourably upon his educated prisoner. Without a shipwreck Paul may well have enjoyed an extremely comfortable passage and had many favours extended to him. Without a shipwreck the captain would have received credit for good navigation, the ship's structure would have been admired for its strength and stability, and the Christian passengers would have concluded that safe and comfortable journeys were the inevitable consequence of human wisdom and technology. But the voyage resulted in disaster and they learned (in Paul's case for the third time) that they were always in the hands of the Lord Who alone holds the keys of life and death. Trials teach us not to depend upon creature aid, or take the guidance, protection, and power of the Lord for granted, but to look to Him in all things.

Yet another purpose of trials is to *guide* the believer. Paul had never planned to go to Malta, and even had he wanted to his escort would not have permitted it. Their ship was bound for Italy where Paul would stand trial in Rome. However, the Lord's will was that Paul would bring the word of salvation to the island of Malta, and His guiding instrument was the hurricane. Some of our greatest trials and upheavals rearrange the circumstances of our lives in a very dramatic way, bringing about changes which we would never have expected or sought, and which we may well have resisted given the opportunity. Without some cataclysmic trial God's purpose, with all its new opportunities, would never have come about.

Sometimes the Lord designs trials or hardships as a means of training His people for even greater trials. The Lord has in mind for us some great privilege of Christian service, but there is a problem, because this role will entail antagonism and opposition from both the devil and the people around us, and we will need to be a person of considerable patience, strength, and trust to win through. If we are not strong enough to cope with the trials it will bring, the Lord may prepare us by toughening us up with smaller pains and troubles. The purpose of these is to deepen our resilience and faith, to reduce our self-concern, and to teach us to pray. The middle-sized trial of next week may well be a kindly preparation for the far greater trial of privileged future service. We see this illustrated by the experience of Paul, because the shipwreck would soon be followed by worse things. The rigours of the sea were preparation for the trials of Rome.

On the brighter side, trials provide unrivalled opportunities for witness and for remarkable encouragement. Those 276 passengers could never have survived *Hurricane Euroclydon* but for the mighty power of God, and the outcome vindicated Paul's words and witness to them, at the same time encouraging Paul, Luke and their fellow believers for the future. Says Newton –

He Who has brought me hitherto,
Will lead me all my journey through.

Trials demonstrate to us the power of God in a way that nothing else can, for when we are reduced to utter helplessness, then the arm of God is seen and the sweetness of His smile is appreciated as at no other time. When life is tranquil and easy and we can cope relatively well by our own strength and ability, our realisation of the power and kindness of God becomes small. Troubles bring the major proofs and assurances of the believer's life.

Of course, trials bring about spiritual advance, whether sanctification for the redeemed or conversion for the lost. I remember a story told to me while on the way to a preaching engagement in California. We were driving through a range of hills not far from Los Angeles some two years after a major earthquake had shaken the area. I learned that an extremely wealthy widow had her mansion in that area where she housed a collection of fine antique china, many items being worth thousands of dollars apiece. This collection was well-known and frequently viewed by experts and other collectors from all over the world, and it was her god, her idol. Though her mansion was supposed to be shock-proof, when the earthquake occurred not many miles away the vibrations of the ground were of just the right frequency and strength to shake the precious antiques to powder, the poor lady watching aghast as every piece cracked and crumbled. Her idol was destroyed, but its destruction brought her to the Lord, because the very next Sunday she went to a service of worship where the Lord spoke to her heart, purging out the love of her idol, and bringing her to repentance. Troubles also purge us of things which have become too important to us, the experience being not so much a punishment as a purging.

Still we have not exhausted the value of trials, because they also have a very special purpose in *testing* us. How do we rate ourselves as believers? Do we think we are making great progress? Do we feel we are exercising faith just as we ought to? Our evaluation of ourselves is seldom objective, but if the Lord sends a trial we see more clearly where we stand as believers, and the quality of our trust in Him. If we go to pieces or behave in a self-pitying or despairing way, then we realise that we have a lot to do to raise the level of our faith (as well as our self-control).

Equally, trials may provide believers with a good indication of the worth or standing of a person under consideration for office in the church, or for appointment to an important task in the work of the Gospel. It may be that the Lord allows trials to come up in the lives of those who seem suitable, and then it will be very clear whether or not they are truly ready. Do they process the affairs of life in a spiritual manner? Let trials test them.

Luke's shipwreck narrative provides important information on the kinds of trial which God may allow to afflict His children. The shipwreck was a fairly long trial, teaching us to expect the same sometimes. Our tendency is to cope bravely with short-lived hardships, but not longer ones. Paul's shipwreck was also a painful, terrifying and faith-challenging trial, and all these elements may be included in the trials which we shall bear. We therefore need to prepare ourselves for a variety of problems such as let-downs, hostility and loss.

In *2 Corinthians 1.8-10* Paul writes:

> **'For we would not, brethren, have you ignorant of our trouble which came to us in Asia, that we were pressed out of measure, above strength, insomuch that we despaired even of life: but we had the sentence of death in ourselves, that we should not trust in ourselves, but in God which raiseth the dead: who delivered us from so great a death, and doth deliver: in whom we trust that he will yet deliver us.'**

Paul does not say what this trial was, but it was so painful that he calls it *so great a death.* He and his companions were brought to the very border of life, to the limit of their endurance, to prove to them that God can snatch His people from the very edge of the precipice, there being no situation too hard for His delivering grace. This experience greatly strengthened them for the future, so that the apostle is left saying, 'in whom we trust that he will yet deliver us'.

We think again of Paul and Luke in their shipwreck on the coast of Malta. In a way Paul was a double prisoner, firstly as a prisoner in the hands of Roman soldiers, and secondly in a vessel destined for shipwreck. Deprived of daylight and food, cold and drenched, his situation was hopeless, yet he and his fellow believers were able to remind themselves that the Lord knew all about it, and possessed power to deliver them. They were confident that God knew where, when and how the end of the trial would come. They would eventually discover that He had even prepared the hearts of 'barbarians' to receive them and care for them. In all trials and tribulations we too should reflect on the fact that the Lord knows exactly how long they will last, how He will provide for our relief, and the purpose or purposes that will be served.

We have already referred to losses incurred by trials, this also being exemplified in the shipwreck of Paul, where the vessel was shorn of cargo, rigging and timbers before becoming a total loss. The passengers lost well-being, comfort, possessions, and time. There is usually a price to be paid in trials and we should not romantically imagine that we will emerge without loss. Hopefully we will lose any idols, along with some rough edges and worldly tendencies, and we may also lose some quite legitimate possessions, comforts, and benefits, because the Lord wants us to derive more of our satisfaction from Him, from His service and Word, and from His spiritual provisions. Trials may therefore make us poorer in wealth or health, but the blessings that we keep are far more precious than anything a trial may take away. And we will continue to enjoy spiritual light, spiritual life, communion, guidance, spiritual safety, the privilege of being used by God, a place in Heaven, and countless additional proofs, assurances and blessings to cheer our hearts. Trials wrongly handled lead to self-pity and bitterness of spirit, whereas rightly responded to they lead to greater appreciation of God's goodness and kindness, and a humble, serving spirit concerned only to be useful to the Lord.

We see this reflected in the behaviour of Paul, the ageing, infirm apostle, when he came to land and was received by the people of Malta. Because of the rain and cold they prepared a fire, and Paul, the venerable apostle, 'gathered a bundle of sticks, and laid them on the fire'. Though wet and exhausted like everyone else, and probably the oldest of the party, and despite possessing the highest educational and cultural background of any, his immediate instinct was to help in the menial task of gathering wood. Paul could so easily have been puffed up because of the greatness of the revelations made to him, and by his outstanding role as a missionary apostle, but trials had served to keep him humble.

C. H. Spurgeon used to be very careful about pride in young men in the early days of his Pastors' College, and letters exist to this day written by Spurgeon to Principal Rogers commenting on prospective students. One assessment which crops up several times in connection with applicants is along these lines: 'Too proud! The devil will get the better of him and he will be no use to the Lord.'

The writer has heard of preachers who say, 'I am a pastor; I am not going to put out chairs or stoop to doing practical things.' There was none of that spirit in Paul. The promise of Christ to apostles exempted him from being killed by serpents, but not from bruising and bleeding. He landed on Malta's shore dazed and weak, but he gathered up the wood so naturally and automatically that it is obvious that this was his normal deportment, and in this he is our example, for the Spirit of God moved him to say – 'Be ye imitators of me.' Paul was always a suitable person for unbelievers to observe, whether they were unconverted travellers, common soldiers, toughened seamen, cultured centurions, or the 'barbarians' of Malta. Trials purge us, deepen us, sanctify us, and humble us, making us more fit to be seen by needy souls.

There is a lesson to be seen even in the way Paul disposed of the viper that 'fastened' on to his hand. He did not flail around to get it off by any means, because it may then have clung to someone else. He was careful to shake it into the fire, and Luke's very precise account is undoubtedly given so that we may conclude that trials – rightly responded to – have the effect of making us more *considerate* of others.

When Paul's enforced stay in Malta was over, and yet another voyage had been completed, he and his companions found themselves approaching Rome, their destination, from where believers had travelled between thirty and forty miles to meet them. When the apostle saw them it is recorded that 'he thanked God, and took courage', showing how he prepared himself for trials of faith. He thanked God for every blessing, being careful to give credit and glory to Him for even the small spiritual comforts. Paul probably feared Rome, the Lord having warned him of the suffering that awaited him, and he may also have feared the thought of spiritual uselessness, anticipating being locked in a cell with no access to either believers or countless lost souls. But the evidence of God's kindness in providing a reception committee, small as it may seem to us, reminded him of the goodness and power of the Gospel, and so he built up his courage.

Once within imperial Rome, 'the centurion delivered the prisoners to the captain of the guard,' but Paul must have felt that events had turned out beyond his hopes and dreams when he was allowed to lodge in a house, with freedom to receive anyone. What did the man of trials do then? He certainly did not rest, because trials had taught him to look for God's purpose in everything, but he immediately took advantage of his measure of liberty to call the leading Jews of Rome to visit him. We may imagine Paul reasoning in himself saying, 'The Lord has arranged matters so that I not only have liberty to ask these Jewish leaders to visit me, but I have military protection should they be as violent toward me as they have been in other places. I must therefore proceed without delay.' The arrangements for an orderly presentation of the Gospel were better than if Paul had been a free man staying in Rome's best inn. How extraordinary are the ways of the Lord, and what glorious spiritual activism we see in Paul! The person who proves the Lord through trials, seeing a higher purpose in everything, learns to read opportunities and to redeem every precious day of life's journey.

Paul remained in Rome for two years and wrote from here the letters to the *Ephesians*, *Philippians*, and *Colossians*, plus the little letter to *Philemon*, after which, it appears, he was acquitted. He then went to Ephesus and on into Macedonia where he wrote *1 Timothy*, and from there he proceeded to Crete where he was again arrested and sent to Rome. From Rome, prior to his execution, he wrote *2 Timothy*. Whether free or at liberty Paul was always mightily used by God. We may think of these profound and lasting prison epistles, or of the growth of the church at Rome, or the witness in high places among the officials of the empire, not to mention Roman garrisons and the household of Caesar. How could Paul be so productive in the midst of such trials? The Lord had prepared him by lesser trials for greater ones, ever strengthening him to cope and to trust.

In all his trials Paul recounted his blessings and built up his joy and peace in believing. Always he reviewed the promises of God and his own past deliverances, provisions and spiritual blessings, recognising a higher divine purpose behind every event. This was his method of viewing and accounting for life's experiences, and it must be ours also, so that every difficulty we meet will serve to increase our usefulness to God, and prepare us for an everlasting spiritual benefit.

[A number of New Testament texts warning believers to expect trials are set out at the end of this book in the Appendix – *Trials – a Christian Perspective.*]

7

Do We Have a Personal Thorn?

'And lest I should be exalted above measure through the abundance of the revelations, there was given to me a thorn in the flesh, the messenger of Satan to buffet me, lest I should be exalted above measure' *(2 Corinthians 12.7).*

UNFORTUNATELY there have always been some preachers who set out to secure for themselves a following by gimmickry or self-projection. Some have been flamboyant show-offs, while others have mastered more subtle forms of professionalism to get admiration and promotion. There are quite a few such 'great ones' around in these days of personality worship and charismatic boasting, and this gives us an insight into a problem which Paul faced long ago. A few self-seeking 'actors' had found it all too easy to overshadow and eclipse the work of Paul, who avoided extravagant oratory in order to communicate as earnestly and plainly as he could. He did not seek to build himself up in the eyes of the people or to impress them with histrionic or dramatic displays. Some said – 'His letters . . . are weighty and powerful; but his bodily presence is weak, and his speech contemptible' *(2 Corinthians 10.10).*

The result was that undiscerning believers, swept along by the phonies, were saying, 'How can Paul be a true apostle? How can someone who is so unimpressive be God's inspired penman?' It became vital for Paul to defend his calling as an apostle. He clearly took no interest in his personal standing, saying, 'Of myself I will not glory,' but it was essential for him to defend his office for if this were discredited then his inspired teaching would be set aside and false teachers would play havoc with the churches.

In his remarkable autobiographical passage of *2 Corinthians 12-13*, Paul breaks a silence of fourteen years to tell how he was caught up into paradise to experience unutterable things. 'I will come,' he says, 'to visions and revelations of the Lord.' After so many years he finds himself compelled to speak of the sublime and distinctive way in which God gave him great revelations, infusing into him truths and doctrines for the New Testament age. Yet the entire passage reflects his acute discomfort at having to speak about himself. Only necessity forces him to speak, and we cannot help but notice the great contrast between Paul and the self-styled 'apostles' of today, with all their showmanship and self-advertisement. Paul is so anxious to avoid the smallest degree of boasting that he adopts an indirect style of description, saying, 'I knew a man in Christ above fourteen years ago.'

In effect he introduces his readers to two people, Paul the ordinary minister and Paul the apostle. It was not as an ordinary man or minister that he received his remarkable experience, but as an appointed apostle of the Lord. Personally he felt he had nothing to boast about or glory in, but he felt compelled to establish his credentials as an apostle and to safeguard the revelations which he had received for the direction of the ongoing churches of Christ.

Paul could not go into the details, and did not know precisely whether he was caught up to Heaven in body or only in spirit. All he knew was that he was ushered into the paradise of God to experience amazing things, and there he received confirmation from the

Lord of his special commission as an inspired penman of God's Word. He heard 'unspeakable words', which means that he heard truths so profound as to be beyond human speech and understanding. He was able to take in and grasp things which may not lawfully be retold on earth, things that will not be known until the day of the Lord. These extra insights and experiences were for Paul alone, perhaps to encourage, consolidate and sustain him in the rigours of his future ministry, but he was not to reveal the details, and never did. However, the apostle was to be God's instrument for writing a large portion of the New Testament, speaking with authority from God, and also suffering enormous resistance and persecution. Therefore God gave him additional knowledge and insight so that he need never be in any doubt about the divine origin of the Truth which he received.

Paul's great reluctance to speak of this unique experience is seen again in the words of *2 Corinthians 12.6*, where he says (we paraphrase), 'Supposing I did want to boast about this experience, I would not be behaving foolishly because my boasting would be true. Nevertheless I abstain from this, in case anyone should form an estimation of me as a person higher than I merit.' The question is, how did Paul manage to maintain his reticence about his secret experience? What enabled him to be so humble, so unflamboyant, so down-to-earth and genuine? What were the special influences in his life which helped him to keep to his modest lifestyle, a manner of life which God intended as an example and pattern for every Christian worker throughout the entire Gospel age?

The chief influence was a painful form of handicap given to him by the Lord of love. The mysterious words of *2 Corinthians 12.7* describe this protective gift of God as something which enabled him to be the most privileged and yet the most unspoilt of men. His own words say: 'And lest I should be exalted above measure through the abundance of the revelations, there was given to me a thorn in the flesh, the messenger of Satan to buffet me, lest I should be exalted above measure.' Twice Paul states that this thorn was given to him so that he would not be over-exalted or too lifted up as the result of his revelations. The apostle could have been unduly elevated by the privilege of his visions and revelations in at least three ways.

First, he could have been lifted up in his own eyes, becoming conceited, self-important and opinionated, even assuming that he alone was worthy to receive such visions.

Secondly, Paul could very easily have been unduly elevated in the estimation of the churches. Had he been entirely fit and bounding in dynamic energy, many may have hero-worshipped or idolised him, regarding him virtually as an angel or a 'saint' in the Catholic sense of the word. They may well have hung to his coat-tails over everything. Instead of taking his epistles along with the rest of Scripture for their study and obedience, they may simply have sought Paul's personal opinion, but God prevented this by means of the thorn, and he was seen to be a frail and needy man with obvious limitations.

Thirdly, Paul, if strong and vigorous, could well have occupied too great a place in the practical work and ministry of the churches, obstructing the emergence of other labourers and helpers. Perhaps Luke the physician would not have been so inclined to travel with him, not to mention others, for what need would a superman have of fellow workers? Why should churches trouble to evangelise, because Paul would be coming soon, able to do everything so much better? But the apostle was not capable of doing everything, and stood in very great need of his fellow labourers all the time. There were times when it seems he could barely operate at all without companions. The achievements of an apostolic superhero were not to provide the atmosphere in which the early churches were cradled. Paul's work was certainly amazing, but the methods and programme of the early churches were to involve the service of all God's people.

Let us go back to the possibility that Paul could have become puffed up with pride and self-confidence by the abundance of the spiritual privileges given to him, forming a completely false opinion of his own worth. He might easily have concluded that God had chosen him because he had superior attainments, having been an accomplished scholar of the law before his conversion. He could well have imagined that his birth and upbringing as a member of an elite Jewish class was also a factor. We are all subject to being adversely affected by our human benefits and so there are lessons for us all in this strange gift of a thorn in the flesh.

Once people begin to think that God needs their brains, qualities, background or breeding, they are on the high road to an arrogance which will quickly make them disdainful and impatient of everyone else. With such ideas germinating in his mind even the godly Paul may have been tempted to look around and notice that not many in the churches had been educated at the feet of Gamaliel as he had been, or passed through any other rabbinical school. If Satan could have made Paul proud of his background and qualities, then the apostle would possibly have trusted his own judgement on matters and become unable to distinguish between God's Word and his own ideas. The time may have come when church leaders would ask him what he thought of this or of that problem, and he would answer briskly and confidently straight out of his own mind. (Tragically, some ministers are like this nowadays.) However, the apostle was required by God to set an example in consulting the Word about everything, and God had His way of helping him to retain a spirit of humble dependence in spite of his lofty calling.

The person who thinks that God is using him because of his intrinsic qualities usually becomes a bully in the Lord's service, and very self-interested, always wanting the credit for the things he does, and always wanting to be noticed. Furthermore, once a person becomes self-interested, the devil makes sure that his other appetites are stirred and stimulated, so that he soon wants a much bigger church or a much nicer home, or a much larger profile in the eyes of

Christians at large. In the light of such dangers the Lord took measures to ensure that the apostle, good and spiritual man as he was, would not be dragged down this dismal route through the weakness of human nature. The thorn in his flesh was pre-eminently protective.

There are other ways in which Christian people may be 'lifted up' and a thorn helps with these also. We may be very greatly blessed with health and prosperity, fulfilment in our employment, and fruitfulness in our witness for the Lord, but these very blessings may make us self-satisfied about our success, and feeling superior to others. We may forget that even in times of success we should be very mindful of the areas of life in which we fail, such as Christian service responsibilities, or other Christian duties. Sometimes our blessings make us too happy to care about our shortcomings and we become complacent about things where we fall short of the mark. Then it is a good thing if some kind of thorn jabs us to bring us down to earth, reminding us of our weaknesses, and restraining self-satisfaction.

Paul's Thorn was an Illness

There is no doubt that Paul's thorn was a physical illness, an unwelcome fact to many charismatic teachers who say Christians should never be sick, and who therefore interpret the thorn as a metaphor for personal enemies or persecutors. They base their claim on the fact that the children of Israel were made to suffer Canaanites as thorns in their sides. But Paul speaks of a singular thorn and specifically says that it was in his flesh. A text which proves conclusively that Paul suffered with his health is found in *Galatians 4.13-14,* where he writes*:* 'Ye know how through infirmity of the flesh I preached the gospel unto you at the first. And my temptation which was in my flesh ye despised not, nor rejected; but received me as an angel of God, even as Christ Jesus.'

Paul's thorn could not possibly refer to his personal enemies for the Lord told Paul that it would not be taken away in answer to prayer, yet Paul repeatedly urges the churches to join him in prayer for deliverance from his enemies, and utters wonderful words of testimony to the effect that he has been delivered.* It is therefore inconceivable that the apostle's irremovable thorn could be his Judaizing enemies, or any other foes as asserted by charismatic healers. Furthermore, Paul's own words make it plain that the thorn was a physical affliction, for he records how the Lord said to him: 'My grace is sufficient for thee: for my strength is made perfect in weakness. Most gladly therefore will I rather glory in my infirmities, that the power of Christ may rest upon me.' He speaks of his infirmities, the Greek word normally indicating strengthlessness, frailty, weakness (physical or moral) and illness.

Do We Have a Personal Thorn?

God's precautionary, preventive thorn is needed in some measure by all believers. We should be clear that it did not just happen, nor was it initiated by the world, the flesh or the devil, but it was something which God initiated and gave, because Paul said that it – 'was

*For example: 'That we may be delivered from unreasonable and wicked men: for all men have not faith' *(2 Thessalonians 3.2)*; 'That I may be delivered from them that do not believe in Judaea; and that my service which I have for Jerusalem may be accepted of the saints' *(Romans 15.31)*; 'For we would not, brethren, have you ignorant of our trouble which came to us in Asia, that we were pressed out of measure, above strength, insomuch that we despaired even of life: but we had the sentence of death in ourselves, that we should not trust in ourselves, but in God which raiseth the dead: who delivered us from so great a death, and doth deliver: in whom we trust that he will yet deliver us' *(2 Corinthians 1.8-10)*; 'Persecutions, afflictions, which came unto me at Antioch, at Iconium, at Lystra; what persecutions I endured: but out of them all the Lord delivered me' *(2 Timothy 3.11)*; 'Notwithstanding the Lord stood with me, and strengthened me; that by me the preaching might be fully known, and that all the Gentiles might hear: and I was delivered out of the mouth of the lion. And the Lord shall deliver me from every evil work, and will preserve me unto his heavenly kingdom: to whom be glory for ever and ever. Amen' *(2 Timothy 4.17-18)*.

given to me'. Some assume it was given by Satan, but, although it became the 'messenger of Satan', it was plainly a gift from God to help him to remain humble, sensitive, dependent on his fellow workers, and aware of his limitations. The thorn was given by God to achieve good ends, and it provided scope for Satan to 'buffet' him (punch him).

Anything which is given to us by God we normally regard as a gift, and hard as it may be to think of the thorn in the flesh as a gift, that is what it was. In His wisdom and kindness God gave a gift which achieved remarkable results. God is the distributor of great grace, yet in His loving wisdom He is also the distributor of thorns to His people, and because Paul knew that his thorn was a gift given by God he was able to face all his troubles with these words (already quoted) – 'Therefore I take pleasure in infirmities, in reproaches, in necessities, in persecutions, in distresses for Christ's sake: for when I am weak, then am I strong.'

What exactly was the apostle's thorn? The Greek word literally means a pointed thing, such as a stake, but undoubtedly a botanical thorn is in mind. It could be a figurative reference to the fiery darts of Satan, his evil suggestions, but these would hardly be a gift from God. They will certainly come, taking advantage of the thorn, but the thorn itself is best understood as a painful, distracting, burdensome kind of illness.

A 'thorn in the flesh' is a remarkable expression for while it withholds details of the illness it says so much about its effects. Sometimes even localised pain such as toothache, earache or a bad blister can totally disrupt life and drain away enthusiasm and vigour, but we believe Paul's thorn to have been considerably worse than these. For all this, a thorn is only a thorn and it cannot crush us, nor can it destroy either body or soul. What God has given, although it may be hard to bear at times, is a limited affliction which cannot destroy either us or our spiritual walk. It is a thorn, not some deadly poison.

Eye disease, sciatica, rheumatism, stammering, leprosy and malaria are all contenders for the identification of Paul's affliction, but the absence of detailed information forces us to think more about the reason why the thorn was given, the result which it achieved, and the spiritual lessons for our own souls.

While Paul's thorn was undoubtedly and literally planted in the body, many of God's people have suffered a thorn in their circumstances, such as John Wesley, who was outrageously harassed by an unbalanced and vicious wife. John Bunyan said that at times the chief cause of distress for him was not his prison cell, but the thought of his poor, blind daughter left without her father. If he would only abandon his principles he would be free and caring for her, and sometimes his pain became so great it was as if his flesh was being torn from his body. Many of the Lord's people have been converted after marriage, and have then encountered great difficulties from their unconverted loved one. A thorn may take many forms.

Do we have a burdensome thorn in our circumstances or in our health? We are not speaking of self-imposed thorns, such as trials and troubles which we get into by choice, because we have been neglectful or foolish or sinful, for these will often be relieved by the re-ordering of our priorities or by putting aside wrong objectives. The question is, do we have an affliction which, for the time being, we are called to endure? If we do not have such a burden at the present time, we may be called to bear with one in the future. In spiritual infancy we are more gently nurtured by the Lord Who bears the lambs in His arms, but later there may arise a measure of affliction in body or circumstances designed to mould, shape and help us. Therefore we must not go to pieces if such a trial comes into our lives because it will be something which God has designed and permitted to minister to us.

A thorn renders us vulnerable to doubting temptations from Satan, and he seizes his opportunity to 'buffet', Paul using a word which literally means – to hit with bare knuckles. A vicious punch is in mind, not an open-handed slap. Satan cannot knock us out, but he can inflict pain and stir up self-pity, as he tries to convince us that our lot is harsh and unreasonable. He may whisper that God is unfair because other believers do not have to put up with such trials, or that it must be someone's fault whom we may blame. Satan may succeed in planting doubts about God's goodness and power, in order to fracture our joy and peace in believing, and he will certainly try to convince us that our situation is hopeless.

Paul's handling of his thorn is instructive, because he pleaded repeatedly to the Lord for its complete removal, but received the famous divine response – 'My grace is sufficient for thee: for my strength is made perfect in weakness.' Paul understood that there would be no imminent cure for his condition but that God had intended it to remain for his long-term spiritual protection.

If we are given a thorn in the flesh it will alter our outlook in many ways. As in the case of Paul, it will deliver us from exalting ourselves, because there is nothing more effective than a painful problem to remind us that we are ordinary, weak, fallible people. It may also cause us to share more with fellow believers and to appreciate them, because afflictions make us feel our need of one another, promoting a spirit of interdependence. Paul's weaknesses doubtless contributed to his appreciation of Barnabas, and later, Silas, Luke, Timothy, Titus and others, and this released the power of God through them also, making them able ministers in the kingdom of God. Paul's suffering probably helped him to be an unusually sensitive, understanding and gentle person, a great listener whose chief delight was to teach, encourage and help others.

Like Paul, we should not be dashed down by trials, sicknesses or circumstances which are not removed despite prayer, because they may be God's gift to us and He knows what He is doing. God is Lord of all, and is therefore the Lord of thorns. It is surely not without significance that the Lord Jesus Christ wore a crown of thorns when He went to Calvary, and has lordship even over these. The thorns in

His crown represent the pangs of everlasting torment which have pierced Him instead of us, and having borne away our punishment and defeated Satan, He has ultimate supervision over our every trial.

Puritan Bishop Hall thought about Paul's thorn, and exclaimed, 'Oh powerful thorn to keep a man's secret for fourteen years!' What gave a man who had been caught up into paradise the humility to utter not a word about it for fourteen years? Strangely, we may think, it was a thorn which produced such virtue. Intransigent trials and problems undoubtedly mellow us and deepen us if we meet them with prayer for help and patience, but we frequently respond to them wrongly. A sickness, instead of leading us to the Lord, may make us bitter, complaining and consumed by self-pity, so that the thorn becomes more deeply embedded and painful. A great need such as a continuing shortage of money may lead to jealousy, meanness and frustration. Other kinds of trial may make us ill-tempered and self-centred. To have a good effect the thorn must be handled in a Christian manner, our attitude being pivotal.

If handled rightly a thorn will produce humility, patience, spiritual dependence, awareness of weaknesses, sensitivity, willingness to share in Christian service, interdependence, lack of self-interest, appreciation of grace, and the constant experiencing of God's sustaining and strengthening power. These are tremendous benefits, and not surprisingly Paul says – 'Most gladly therefore will I rather glory in my infirmities, that the power of Christ may rest upon me. Therefore I take pleasure in infirmities, in reproaches, in necessities, in persecutions, in distresses for Christ's sake: for when I am weak, then am I strong' *(2 Corinthians 12.9-10).*

The words which Paul uses, 'that the power of Christ may rest upon me', are an unusual and beautiful figure of speech. The word translated 'rest' may be rendered more literally, 'may spread its tent over me'. To prove a person through trial is God's favourite method of sanctifying, and to know this is a great source of encouragement and assurance to us. Blessing and instrumentality repeatedly come through experiences and burdens which we think are disadvantages and frailties, but God surprises us and we say, 'I never thought my disadvantage would lead to this,' and, 'surely the Lord enabled me!' The renowned Bishop Hall may well have said, 'Oh powerful thorn which causes the power of Christ to spread its tent over us!' The well-loved and favourite verse of so many believers provides a perfect summary of our chapter on thorns:–

> **'And we know that all things work together for good to them that love God, to them who are the called according to his purpose'** *(Romans 8.28).*

In addition, a magnificent hymn of Josiah Conder's supplies a prayer for times of trial and for thorns:–

Heavenly Father! to Whose eye
Future things unfolded lie;
Through the desert where I stray,
Let Thy counsels guide my way.

Lead me not, for flesh is frail,
Where the fiercest trials assail;
Leave me not, in darkened hour,
To withstand the tempter's power.

Lord, uphold me day by day;
Shed a light upon my way;
Guide me through perplexing snares;
Care for me in all my cares.

Should Thy wisdom, Lord, decree
Trials long and sharp for me,
Pain or sorrow, care or shame,
Father, glorify Thy name.

Let me neither faint nor fear,
Knowing still that Thou art near;
In the course my Saviour trod,
Travelling home to Thee, my God!

8

Is My Trouble a Reproof or a Trial?

'Ye have forgotten the exhortation which speaketh unto you as unto children, My son, despise not thou the chastening of the Lord, nor faint when thou art rebuked of him' *(Hebrews 12.5).*

SOME CHRISTIANS think that all severe trials must be chastisements from God, while others exclude this possibility altogether. The text quoted above warns us not to overlook the possibility of discipline, but how can we tell if we are under discipline? After all, countless trials and hardships are not disciplinary, as we have seen from the experience of Paul the prisoner of the Lord. It was God's will that he should be arrested and imprisoned so that a great witness would be brought to pass. Besides having been shipwrecked (three times) Paul also suffered terrible floggings, hunger, thirst, stoning, and a persistent painful illness, but he said, 'I will glory of the things which concern mine infirmities.' Clearly he did not regard these experiences as punishments or chastisements from the Lord, for he would surely not have gloried in being punished by God. Paul's situation proves that even the most extreme troubles must not be too readily regarded as a mark of God's disapproval. When the great missionary apostle lost his liberty to preach, suffering instead the brutality of Roman captivity, some may have thought there was some dark and guilty secret in Paul's life, but it was not so. How could Paul be so sure that he was not under discipline, and how may we tell whether or not our trials are a form of punishment? The answer is given in *Hebrews 12.5-11* where we learn the basic principles of God's discipline. Quoting *Proverbs 3.11*, the writer says, 'My son, despise not thou the chastening of the Lord, nor faint when thou art rebuked of him.' From this we observe that the Lord's harder disciplines always follow gentler chastening, the words showing a gradation from something mild enough to be ignored, to a severe rebuke.

If, therefore, a believer who is experiencing tranquillity is suddenly stricken down by a serious setback or illness without prior warning, this will not be a discipline from God. He is the perfect father, and not like a parent who suddenly flies into a rage, rushes up to a child and administers a furious thrashing. When we come under His discipline we will know why, for our conscience will be stirred at the same time. One way of telling if we are under discipline is to ask – Have I resisted a history of milder chastening? Has there been wilful continuance in known sin, or avoidance of some known duty? Has there been a failure to meet with the Lord even though the conscience has been repeatedly touched about the matter? A painful rebuke will always be preceded by the stirring of conscience and a period of progressively firmer chastenings and warnings. What form do these 'milder' chastenings take?

In *Hebrews 12.12-13* we see that God's discipline is often first applied to spiritual blessings and enjoyments. 'Wherefore lift up the hands which hang down, and the feeble knees; and make straight paths for your feet, lest that which is lame be turned out of the way; but let it rather be healed.' Although the language of sickness and twisted joints is used here, it is obviously intended as a picture of spiritual feebleness because the sufferers are able to straighten themselves out, presumably by prompt repentance and rededication.

This kind of chastening involves the loss of spiritual graces and benefits, so that we become enfeebled as Christians, the Lord drawing a cloud across the heavens and restricting our spiritual blessings so that we lose our enjoyment of prayer, ministry and fellowship. Christian service becomes irksome, and we feel a heaviness of spirit, stumbling constantly. If assurance and communion with God are precious to us we become alarmed and exercised about our sinful conduct. If we are insensitive to conscience when such a discipline comes then a stronger rebuke may be necessary.

Another form of preliminary discipline employed by the Lord is felt when He moves to frustrate our worldly aspirations or covetous idols. When Jonah ran from the Lord in disobedience God frustrated his purpose, obstructing the course he took and bringing many troubles into his life. Take the case of a believer who buys an unnecessarily luxurious and expensive new car, polishes it three times a week, lavishes accessories upon it, parks it where he can relish the sight of it from his window, and makes it the object of his delight day after day. It would not surprise us at all to hear that the precious idol had been smashed or scarred in an accident, because the Lord often frustrates the worldly delights and selfish aspirations of those He loves. He is very likely to dislocate worldly objectives as a means of bringing us to our senses.

An example is provided by the Jews of old, who took possession of the promised land flowing with milk and honey, and promptly devoted themselves to the pursuit of prosperity and pleasure. They tilled and worked the ground to fulfil their covetous desires, working on the Sabbath day and abusing God's rules for their tenancy. Consequently the Lord allowed the land to be overrun by the Babylonians. If we are devoted overmuch to our careers or personal aggrandisement, it may be that our well-laid plans unaccountably begin to go wrong. We may be inexplicably overlooked in promotion, or redundancy may loom, exploding all our self-serving aspirations, yet the Lord may not have laid a finger on us in terms of sickness. These things are not necessarily discipline, but they may be, and if they are we will know why.

In both warfare and medical science there is the problem of how to hit a target or a disease without hideous side-effects. We read of medical researchers targeting their drugs more accurately on offending cells, and of smart bombs designed to avoid civilian casualties. When God's ancient people became covetous He first afflicted their wealth, saying, 'I smote you with blasting and with mildew and with hail in all the labours of your hands; yet ye turned not to me.' Have we ignored the voice of conscience and continued in sin despite some initial discipline of the Lord? Have we consequently forfeited spiritual blessings, or suffered a selective discipline of God against our worldly schemes? If so, and we continue to push ahead unrepentant, we are in danger of yet more serious forms of correction, because God loves us and will not let us destroy our spiritual lives.

The unchastised person (as *Hebrews 12.8* declares) is surely unconverted, whatever his claims. In *Hebrews 12.6*, we read: 'For whom the Lord loveth he chasteneth, and scourgeth every son whom he receiveth,' assuring us that the Lord's discipline has a loving basis. It may have to be severe in cases of extreme and protracted sin, but it is never cruel or hostile in character.

Some of the trials in this fallen, cursed world are much too cruel to be chastisements sent from the Lord. If, for example, a believer were to be viciously attacked and raped, that would surely not be a discipline designed and sent from God. In the event of such a thing happening to a believer our utmost sympathy and support would be called for, and the sufferer should not for a moment believe it to be a chastisement. Someone may protest that God used the murderous activities of the Babylonians to discipline His people, but the comparison is not appropriate. The Jews, after a long period of repeated warnings, had (as a nation) rejected and abandoned the protective arm of the Lord, and thus exposed themselves to the cruelties of the ancient world. In the same way a longstanding, extreme backslider may be exposed to the cruelties of life as a part of restorative discipline, but, in the ordinary course of events, God's discipline is not cruel in character. If we are shaken by a cruel tragedy, trial or illness, we may, speaking generally, be safe in assuming that it is not a divine discipline. God, of course, in His sovereignty permits all things that happen, and will give wonderful grace to bear them, but we are speaking here of divine acts of fatherly discipline.

We read much nowadays of people ill-treating their children, and excusing themselves by blaming the irritating behaviour of the child. What sort of discipline is this? It is not discipline but ill-temper and cruelty, and the God of infinite holiness cannot behave in that way. We may, therefore, be confident that fearfully disabling accidents, mental health breakdowns (where the most precious gift of reason is dislocated), and very major tragedies, would not be employed by God as the means of chastening His people.

Clearly the Lord does at times use sickness as a means of reproving His people, Paul stating in *1 Corinthians 11.30* that many Corinthian church members had succumbed to 'weak and sickly' ailments because they had spurned the duties of sincere self-examination and repentance. There were evidently a number of proud, self-satisfied, antinomian, presumptuous, unrepenting believers in Corinth. The apostle elaborates on this through the epistle, identifying the following sinful attributes represented in that church:– 'For ye are yet carnal; now ye are full, now ye are rich; there is fornication among you, and ye are puffed up, and have not rather mourned; ye do wrong, and defraud, and that your brethren.' He urges them to judge or assess themselves in order to avoid being 'chastened of the Lord'. Certainly God may visit His people with ailments for wilful and protracted refusal to live a sincere Christian life, but with what kind of sickness? The Corinthian backsliders suffered *weakness*, meaning the loss of vigour and strength. This does not necessarily refer to drastic and irreversible disease, but to afflictions which remove the well-being of the sufferer and frustrate the uninhibited enjoyment of the backslidden state. They were conditions which suited the Lord's objective, namely, to bring sinning Christians to consider the empty formalism and hypocrisy of their lives, and to cry out to Him for forgiveness and help.

Some, it appears, had become so fixed in their ways, and were setting such an appalling example to others, that the Lord found it necessary to remove them from the scene, and take them home, but nothing we read in *1 Corinthians 11* supports the idea that the more cruel, disabling, frightening and painful forms of affliction were chastisements sent from God.

James 5.14-15 teaches that sin may sometimes be the reason why a believer is suffering from an illness which confines him to bed. How may we know if our bedridden condition is a discipline from God? We should ask ourselves whether we are scriptural candidates for such an affliction, using questions such as these:–

(1) Have I spurned self-examination?

(2) Have I ignored my sin, and wilfully continued in it?

(3) Have I pretended to be walking spiritually though I have long since left meaningful repenting, prayer and dedication to the Lord?

(4) Have I become a hypocritical worshipper, spiritually uninvolved even during the Lord's Supper?

(5) Has the Lord already punished me with lighter punishments and afflictions which I have knowingly and obstinately ignored?

(6) Have I become 'sickly', and been in that state for some while, still refusing to search my heart and change my hypocritical ways?

If these questions must be answered in the affirmative, there is every likelihood that an illness may be a discipline from the Lord, but even in these circumstances the suffering will not be irreversible.

If, however, I have repented of my sin and sought the Lord's help to avoid recurrence, and returned to walking humbly before Him, and if I have not been knowingly disciplined in a 'lighter' way, then my illness is unlikely to be a punishment from God. We should note that illness is not the Lord's only way of correcting wayward believers. Most sick Christians are not under discipline, and most Christians who come under discipline are reproved by means other than sickness. (This rather sweeping assertion is based only on pastoral observation.)

The questions just suggested about illness may equally be applied to any serious and perplexing trial. We will know if our spiritual lives have collapsed into a hypocritical show, with no sincere confession of sin, and with serious misdeeds and even feuds perpetuated, indicating that a trial could well be a discipline.

Another test which may be applied to determine whether an illness or trial is a reproof from the Lord, is whether the problem is lifted when we repent. In *Hebrews 12.11* we read: 'Now no chastening for the present seemeth to be joyous, but grievous: nevertheless afterward it yieldeth the peaceable fruit of righteousness unto them which are exercised thereby.' The implication is that the trial comes to an end after repentance. The affliction is 'for the present' (or 'for the moment'), and then there is a peaceful conclusion. When the punishments of the Lord lead to genuine heart-searching and repentance, then mercy and restoration follow. Therefore, if a suffering believer sincerely repents and rededicates himself to the Lord, but the trial continues, the ongoing trial may not be a punishment from the Lord, but a trial to be borne by the kindly help of the Lord. Every trial should have the effect of pulling us up short to examine our hearts, but afflictions which are specifically designed by the Lord to chastise us will be taken away once they have served their purpose. This is also implied in the emphatic words of forgiveness in *James 5.15*, where the healing of a sinful sufferer is mentioned.

Does this mean that there is never an ongoing price to pay for sin?

To answer this we must distinguish between punishment and loss of privilege, because sin may certainly have long-term implications. God may design a painful punishment to bring us to conviction and repentance, coupled with a loss of privilege (for example, the loss of certain Christian service opportunities) as a long-term consequence. An obvious example would be that of an adulterous minister, who could be forgiven by the Lord, but not returned to pastoral service. The same would be true of the loss of some idolised possession. The Lord forgives, but this should not be taken as licence to bring the object back.

It is necessary to stress that God's punishments do not continue beyond the point of repentance, as many believers suffer greatly because they think that God goes on punishing. Some feel that for years God has continued to afflict them because of an old sin, long since repented of, but God does not act in this way. He would never keep up a hostile vendetta against His beloved children. The words of *Hebrews 12.6* are strangely encouraging on this point: 'For whom the Lord loveth he chasteneth, and scourgeth every son whom he receiveth.' This *scourging* is literally a whipping, a punishment which could be severe in Bible times, but was still brief compared with imprisonment. However harsh, it was not usually fatal, and the Roman version was confined to less than twenty minutes. It was short, sharp, and soon over. It was certainly humiliating, being administered in public so that the man who was whipped could no longer maintain a superior stance, pretending to be above the strictures of society. But the whipping analogy indicates the transient nature of God's reproofs.

We may conclude with a great encouragement from the *Hebrews* passage. 'Whom the Lord loveth he chasteneth, and scourgeth every son whom he receiveth.' The one He *receives* is the person He owns, accepts, takes into His family, and cares for. The verse in *Proverbs* from which this is quoted calls this person 'the son in whom he delighteth'. God reproves only the people in whom He delights. 'If ye endure chastening,' says the text, 'God dealeth with you as with sons.'

To 'endure' chastening means that we accept it, confessing with a meek spirit, 'I know I have done these things.' It may not always be a sinful deed for which we are reproved, but irresponsibility or laziness or neglect of duties. It may be a sin of omission as much as a sin of commission, but if we face up to it and say, 'Lord, help me to be different; help me to be better; I deserved this rebuke; I will not recoil in pride, but accept it and respond to it,' then this is a sure sign that we really are children of God.

Do we accept chastening? Do we accept all the standards by which we ought to live? Do we have a sanctifying process going on in our lives? Are we correctable? Do we repent? Do we reform? Do we cry out for help? Do we strive to do better? If this sanctifying process is being carried on in our lives, according to the assurances of this *Hebrews* passage, we are the Lord's; we are regenerate; we belong to Him.

Chastening should not only correct us, but move us to thankfulness to God for His fatherly care. We should feel, 'I have been dealt with by the Lord! How kind He is to me! He is the perfect Father. He has delivered me from great error in pulling me up short.' May the chastenings that we receive be gentle ones only, because we respond to them, never needing to have the sharp knock which comes if we refuse God's progressive sanctifying of our lives.

Getting Assurance

– PART FOUR –

9

Gaining and Keeping Assurance

'We desire that every one of you do shew the same diligence to the full assurance of hope unto the end' *(Hebrews 6.11).*

ASSURANCE IS ONE of those subjects which gave rise to remarkable treatments by the great Bible expositors of the 17th century, the Puritans. Best of all, they compressed their chief conclusions into several superb statements in the *Westminster Confession of Faith* (1646), echoed in the *Second London Baptist Confession* (1677 and 1689).

This chapter will first explain several classic sentences from the two confessions, then review foundational assurance texts from the New Testament. The next chapter will say more about how to obtain and retain assurance. The following quotations are taken from the 18th chapter common to both the *Westminster* and *Baptist Confessions*, the chapter being entitled, 'Of Assurance of Grace and Salvation'. The first clearly states the availability of assurance:–

'Such as truly believe in the Lord Jesus and love Him in sincerity,

> **endeavouring to walk in all good conscience before Him, may in this life be certainly assured that they are in the state of grace and may rejoice in the hope of the glory of God.'**

More will need to be said about that little word 'may' because it implies that some converted people are not 'certainly assured'. Who fails to obtain assurance – many people or few? We take the view that some new converts may wait for a while before being certain of salvation, while a very small minority of Christians, sadly, never seem to gain assurance. The confessions go on to provide a brilliantly helpful summary of the sources (or supports) of assurance, the first being . . .

> **'the divine truth of the promises of salvation'** ***(Westminster)*****, or, 'the blood and righteousness of Christ revealed in the Gospel'** ***(Baptist)*****.**

These days believers look for clear evidence of salvation in their lives as the first vital source of assurance, and are surprised to find that the Reformers and the Puritans put evidence in second place. They saw that the Bible puts something else in first place, insisting that the first source or foundation of assurance is *our own faith* in the doctrines of the Gospel, and particularly in the blood and righteousness of Christ. Thinking in line with Scripture, they taught that saving faith given by the Holy Spirit consists of two components: (1) a certainty that the Gospel is true, and (2) a certainty that God's promises of salvation will be kept in our case, as we embrace Christ. Assurance begins here, they taught, because this kind of saving faith is sure of what it believes. If we are certain about these two 'components' of saving faith then we are already assured, having been given clear convictions about the Gospel and the work of Christ, and having trusted in them with our whole heart. In other words, a great measure of assurance comes with the gift of saving faith. Now we may proceed to the second source of assurance identified in the confessions as . . .

> **'the inward evidence of those graces of the Spirit'.**

As we recognise the evidence of salvation within us (the receiving of a new nature and the process of sanctification which has begun), we may be confirmed in our certainty that God has brought us to salvation.

To repeat these two aspects of assurance, *firstly*, the Holy Spirit opens our eyes and gives saving faith so that we become convinced of the truth of Gospel promises and embrace Christ; *secondly*, we are able to see the fruits of salvation in our own lives. To see the evidences of a changed nature within us is precious, but the first ground of assurance must always be – 'God has brought me to see and believe and receive the Gospel with all my heart.' That precious flame of certainty must be kept alive by appreciation of and thanksgiving for the Gospel and the person and work of Christ.

The third basis of assurance noted in the confessions is –

> **'the testimony of the Spirit of adoption, witnessing with our spirits that we are the children of God'.**

This refers *firstly* to the work of the Spirit as He amplifies the certainty we get from the first two sources; *secondly* as He increases our understanding and certainty when we reflect upon the Word of God; and *thirdly,* as we receive a stream of evidence in the course of the Christian life, through answers to prayer (particularly in time of trial and when we are engaging in service for the Lord).

The 'testimony of the Spirit of adoption' (from *Romans 8.15-16*) has been hijacked by those who teach that believers may obtain from the Spirit a directly imparted, special, ecstatic sensation of assurance of the kind sometimes claimed. The witness of the Spirit is certainly a wonderful sense of assurance, but it comes alongside appreciation and gratitude for the Word, for salvation, and for answered prayer. It is given in the context of spiritual family life ('Spirit of *adoption*'), that is, God dealing with us as a father deals with his children, providing for us day by day.

We now turn to a selection of Scripture passages referring to assurance, beginning with those which speak of the reality of this blessing, and our duty to pursue and maintain it. We appeal to readers to review these texts because they are so helpful if we are to have a really clear view of the wonderful blessing of assurance.

Texts Teaching that Assurance is for All Believers

> **'I am the good shepherd, and know my sheep, and am known of mine. As the Father knoweth me, even so know I the Father: and I lay down my life for the sheep'** ***(John 10.14-15).***

– The Lord's words make no exceptions, implying that all believers will have available to them full certainty in their perception of Him, by faith.

> **'That which we have seen and heard declare we unto you, that ye also may have fellowship with us: and truly our fellowship is with the Father, and with his Son Jesus Christ. And these things write we unto you, that your joy may be full'** ***(1 John 1.3-4).***

> **'These things have I written unto you that believe on the name of the Son of God; that ye may know that ye have eternal life'** ***(1 John 5.13).***

– There is no question in the mind of the apostle John that all believers *should* enjoy a confident sense of being in happy fellowship with the Father and with the Son. The reason for John's letter is that some believers evidently did not enjoy this assurance to the full. A lack of assurance is supposed, and this needed to be corrected.

Texts Teaching that Assurance Accompanies Faith

> **'In whom we have boldness and access with confidence by the faith of him** ***[ie: by faith in him]' (Ephesians 3.12).***

– This text shows that assurance accompanies faith in Christ and His Gospel (the first source of assurance given in the confessions quoted earlier). If we consciously and intelligently affirm our faith in Him in our prayers and thoughts, thanking God for the truths on which our souls rest, both in public worship and personal devotions, the Spirit will wonderfully magnify our certainty. (Hymn singing is of immense value for rehearsing and affirming distinctively New Testament truths and promises.) Because faith is a gift from God, we may say that assurance also is a gift, but clearly it is also a duty to exercise faith, and so we must conclude that assurance is both a gift and a duty.

> **'For the which cause I also suffer these things: nevertheless I am not ashamed: for I know whom I have believed, and am persuaded that he is able to keep that which I have committed unto him against that day'** *(2 Timothy 1.12).*

– Here is assurance grounded firmly on the promises of the Gospel, the person and work of Christ, and His absolute integrity and infallibility. The first and highest source of assurance is to place one's faith in these things, and to reflect on them, value them and affirm them. Because the apostle was totally persuaded of them, his heart was assured.

> **'For I am persuaded** *[convinced utterly]*, **that neither death, nor life, nor angels, nor principalities, nor powers, nor things present, nor things to come, nor height, nor depth, nor any other creature, shall be able to separate us from the love of God, which is in Christ Jesus our Lord'** *(Romans 8.38-39).*

– Paul's certainty here is grounded on the mighty love of God, Who has made infallible promises to all who trust in Him, and has sent Christ to pay a terrible price for our souls. Reflection on this theme forms, strengthens and sustains assurance.

> **'. . . that by two immutable things, in which it was impossible for God to lie, we might have a strong consolation** *[indicating certainty and assurance]*, **who have fled for refuge to lay hold upon the hope set before us: which hope we have as an anchor of the soul, both sure and stedfast, and which entereth into that within the veil'** *(Hebrews 6.18-19).*

– In these verses assurance is based on the embracing of promises about future glory, and the active exercise of trust in them.

> **'Having therefore, brethren, boldness to enter into the holiest by the blood of Jesus, by a new and living way, which he hath consecrated for us, through the veil, that is to say, his flesh; and having an high priest over the house of God; let us draw near with a true heart in full assurance of faith'** *(Hebrews 10.19-22).*

– To approach God with faith in Christ's all-availing blood, is to have assurance.

> **'And we know that the Son of God is come, and hath given us an understanding, that we may know him that is true, and we are in him that is true, even in his Son Jesus Christ. This is the true God, and eternal life'** ***(1 John 5.20).***

– These words elevate faith in the Gospel promises as the chief basis of assurance. As we rest our souls on these truths, affirm them and rejoice in them, our conviction, confidence and certainty is consolidated and deepened.

> **'. . . whose house are we, if we hold fast the confidence and the rejoicing of the hope firm unto the end'** ***(Hebrews 3.6).***

– 'Hope' means anticipation (of Heaven). It is clear in this verse that there is something we must do to maintain assurance throughout life, and this is to 'hold fast', always appreciating and rejoicing in the doctrines of the Gospel.

> **'Seeing therefore it remaineth that some must enter therein, and they to whom it was first preached entered not in because of unbelief . . . Let us therefore come boldly unto the throne of grace, that we may obtain mercy, and find grace to help in time of need'** ***(Hebrews 4.6, 16).***

– The believer should be clothed with a boldness (or confidence) in his approach to God in prayer, and this arises from believing. As faith is kept alive by continuing reflection and appreciation, assurance grows. We should note that none of these texts offer a form of assurance imparted *directly* to Christians by the Spirit. This blessing comes as we believe, hold fast, come boldly, and lay hold, all these being descriptions of the exercise of intelligent faith in Christ.

Texts Teaching Assurance from Inward Evidence

The following texts show that assurance is helped by the believer recognising the evidence of salvation and sanctification in his own life. This is the second ground and source of assurance mentioned in the confessions – the inward evidence of graces of the Spirit. Many texts could be quoted to show this source of assurance, of which the following are key examples.

'Examine yourselves, whether ye be in the faith; prove your own selves. Know ye not your own selves, how that Jesus Christ is in you, except ye be reprobates?' *(2 Corinthians 13.5.)*

– Paul virtually says, 'Can you not see in yourselves the evidence that Christ is at work in you?' If we are saved we can see the evidence of a tender conscience, love for Christ and other signs of the new nature.

'And hereby we do know that we know him, if we keep his commandments. He that saith, I know him, and keepeth not his commandments, is a liar, and the truth is not in him. But whoso keepeth his word, in him verily is the love of God perfected: hereby know we that we are in him' *(1 John 2.3-5).*

– This passage speaks very clearly about assurance being derived from the evidence of grace within the believer. Here is a test of spiritual life from which we may draw great encouragement. If there is serious concern in our hearts to live a godly life, and if our consciences are tender so that the Word of God challenges our behaviour, then we carry within us an indication that we are children of God.

'And he that keepeth his commandments dwelleth in him, and he in him. And hereby we know that he abideth in us, by the Spirit which he hath given us' *(1 John 3.24).*

– This verse links the evidence of our concern for holiness with the work of the Spirit. It is the Spirit Who so touches our consciences with hungerings and thirstings for advance, and these are evidences that we are saved. *1 John 4.13* confirms the point:–

'Hereby know we that we dwell in him, and he in us, because he hath given us of his Spirit.'

'He that loveth his brother abideth in the light, and there is none occasion of stumbling in him' *(1 John 2.10).*

– This is the first of several verses in the epistle showing that the special bond between true believers is sure evidence of grace. *1 John 3.10* combines this and the previous point:–

'In this the children of God are manifest, and the children of the

devil: whosoever doeth not righteousness is not of God, neither he that loveth not his brother.'

'We know that we have passed from death unto life, because we love the brethren. He that loveth not his brother abideth in death' *(1 John 3.14).*

– Both of the preceding verses confirm the family bond as an evidence of salvation and an encouragement to assurance. Can we say, 'For all my faults, weaknesses, foolish grievances and unworthy attitudes, I know that I have a far greater bond with fellow believers than is possible with non-believers'? If so, then there is surely grace in the heart. The theme continues in *1 John 3.17* and *19*:

'But whoso hath this world's good, and seeth his brother have need, and shutteth up his bowels of compassion from him, how dwelleth the love of God in him? . . . And hereby we know that we are of the truth, and shall assure our hearts before him.'

Texts Teaching Assurance by the Witness of the Spirit

The third ground or source of assurance listed in the confessions is that which comes as the Holy Spirit witnesses with our spirits that we are the children of God. The Holy Spirit does not give feelings of assurance independently of (i) our faith in His Word and the joy we derive from it; (ii) our appreciation of the transforming work carried out within us; and (iii) our proving of the Lord in prayer. The witness of the Spirit operates alongside faith and 'inward evidence' in a way we shall describe. *Romans 8.15-16* provides the words that explicitly mention the witness of the Holy Spirit in assurance:

'For ye have not received the spirit of bondage again to fear; but ye have received the Spirit of adoption, whereby we cry, Abba, Father. The Spirit itself beareth witness with our spirit, that we are the children of God.'

– These verses refer to the certainty of belonging to the Lord that begins at the time of conversion. We receive from the Spirit the confidence to pray, along with a certainty that we are heard by our heavenly Father. Then, as we prove the Lord in prayer, frequently receiving remarkable deliverances and powerful help, and as we study and reflect on spiritual truths, the Spirit often gives us tremendously appreciative and clear views of the kindness of our God and Saviour, and our hearts overflow with wonder, love and praise. If we do not pray much, or reflect on the truths of redemption, and fail to praise God for these things, the Spirit will not work in His special way to seal them on our hearts. He chooses to amplify what is engaging our minds, bearing witness 'with our spirit'. Paul describes in a similar way the Spirit's work in assurance in *Romans 5.5*:

> **'And hope *[anticipation]* maketh not ashamed; because the love of God is shed abroad in our hearts by the Holy Ghost which is given unto us.'**

– This hope (of Heaven) is a profound expectation, which moves the heart and at times causes it to soar. We have repeatedly mentioned that some people want the blessing of the Spirit to be a kind of out-of-the-body sensation, imparted directly to the soul, but it is a magnified realisation of Christ's love and work for us imparted as we reflect on the Truth, and on God's dealings with us. Why should we seek alternative mystical sensations which have no connection with the Word and with the walk of faith? When the Holy Spirit impresses the things of Christ on our hearts, our assurance and peace is very great, for Paul says that God's love is 'shed abroad' or poured abundantly into our hearts. This is undoubtedly the same as the witness of the Spirit in *Romans 8.15-16*, deepening our appreciation of the things seen with the eye of faith.

In *2 Corinthians 1.21-22* we are introduced to the term, the sealing of the Spirit:–

> **'Now he which stablisheth us with you in Christ, and hath anointed us, is God; who hath also sealed us, and given the earnest of the Spirit in our hearts.'**

This sealing appears again in *Ephesians 1.13-14* –

> **'In whom ye also trusted, after that ye heard the word of truth, the gospel of your salvation: in whom also after that ye believed, ye were sealed with that holy Spirit of promise, which is the earnest of our**

> **inheritance until the redemption of the purchased possession, unto the praise of his glory.'**

– Paul does not speak here as though such assurance is the rare attainment of a privileged few, but clearly states that all the Ephesian believers were sealed from the time of conversion. The sealing work of the Spirit is called an 'earnest' (or foretaste or guarantee) of Heaven, and accompanies our believing and embracing the promises of the Gospel. These verses say that the Holy Spirit works with our faith, giving us a far brighter eye of faith. No wonder our feelings, acting in response, sometimes soar. The Spirit gives and inspires our faith in the first place, then as we exercise it, believing in Christ, He blesses it and endows it with even greater insight and appreciation.

Ephesians 3.16-19 ties together the experience of glorious certainty with an understanding of the love of Christ, the apostle praying –

> **'That he would grant you, according to the riches of his glory, to be strengthened with might by his Spirit in the inner man; that Christ may dwell in your hearts by faith; that ye, being rooted and grounded in love, may be able to comprehend with all saints what is the breadth, and length, and depth, and height; and to know the love of Christ, which passeth knowledge, that ye might be filled with all the fulness of God.'**

– These verses follow Paul's great statements about preaching the unsearchable riches of Christ. They are about the *ongoing* work of the Spirit in the life of the believer. In view is the happy calling of the believer to learn and glory in the greatness of the person and work of Christ. First, Paul prays for the Spirit to help them to be filled with love for Christ (as they hear about Him), then to help them understand all the love of Christ, and to cause this knowledge to fully engage and satisfy them. The last of these, which we may call wonderful assurance, arises from both learning of Christ, and experiencing His power in the Christian life, through His overruling guidance and numerous answers to prayer. We know the love of Christ not only from what He has done in redemption, but also by what He continues to do, in His amazing kindness, in our lives. We note yet again that the deep certainty and joy (which is Christ dwelling in the heart) does not fall upon us as a sensational experience directly imparted by the Spirit. It comes as the Spirit strengthens our faith and love for Christ, enlarging our 'comprehension' of the things we believe, giving us a fuller sight of His greatness and love, and filling us with gratitude for the outworking of that love in our lives.

* * *

All three sources of assurance named in the confessions have been represented in these verses. They are:

(1) certainty that the Gospel is true, and that God's promise of salvation will be kept in our case;

(2) recognition of the evidence of a new nature and other marks of salvation in our lives, together with the implementation of a sanctification process;

(3) the blessing of the Spirit in firstly enlarging our sight and appreciation of the blessings in the first two categories, and then providing a flow of evidence in answer to prayer, especially in times of trial and service for the Lord.

10

Assurance and Gratitude

'Rooted and built up in him, and stablished in the faith, as ye have been taught, abounding therein with thanksgiving' *(Colossians 2.7).*

STRONG ASSURANCE, as we have noted through these chapters, is to be maintained by regular affirmation of great wonders of the faith in our prayers, praise and reflection. Even the believer who has been saved many years and has the doctrines of salvation etched indelibly in his mind should include the practice of *affirmation* in devotions, regularly reviewing great truths with wholehearted thanksgiving. If we believingly and feelingfully enumerate before God our dependence upon the person and work of Christ, our hearts will remain assured and the Spirit will deepen our appreciation of them and the strength of our convictions. As our soul 'witnesses' in affirmation and wonder, the Holy Spirit witnesses to us of the truthfulness and glory of these things.

This leads us to refer again to the great helpfulness of hymns which plainly affirm all the New Testament doctrines of redemption. If hymns are carefully selected in worship, then worshippers may regularly name the attributes of God, review the work of Christ on Calvary, glory in His great love and amazing grace, and give thanks for so many other great truths of redemption, not to mention the Lord's promises and plans. As the faith is affirmed and praise abounds so certainty and assurance will abound also. Hymns of worship based upon New Testament light give glory to God and at the same time strengthen assurance in accordance with the link between affirmation and assurance seen in the texts which were reviewed earlier. In hymns we articulate regularly our total dependence upon redemption foundations, our faith is exercised, and the things about which we have sung live in our hearts long after the end of the service. If we do not sing with sincerity and love about our Lord and Saviour Jesus Christ in New Testament language we lose a large and precious department of the kind of 'affirmation' on which assurance thrives. At conversion we expressed our reliance upon the blood and righteousness of Christ as revealed in the Gospel, and we must go on affirming that reliance in prayer and worship until the great day comes when we shall see Him.

It is a sad situation when a believer under pressure of trials, or distracted by earthly cares, prays and worships without consciously deriving comfort from these truths of salvation, for this practice is the first and chief source of certainty. We must affirm all precious aspects of Truth, by restating our belief in them, our love of them, and our dependence upon them. Whenever we find great truths during our personal reading of the Word, we should pause, reflect, and thank God for them, telling Him how much we believe them and admire them.

The first piece of advice we give to the believer who has an assurance problem is to bring to a halt the endless question, 'Am I saved, or am I not?' by encouraging the exercise of faith in reaffirming the truths that the Spirit has already written upon the heart, expressing love for them, and drawing comfort from them. The believer should set aside the devil's impertinent questioning of his standing, and apply himself to his first and highest duty, that of affirmation, gratitude and thanksgiving. Then assurance will certainly revive. Satan may suggest that this procedure is merely a form of self-brainwashing, adopted to produce a programmed, artificial certainty, but it is not. It is not the vain, mindless repetition of ideas imposed upon the believer, but an intelligent, appreciative activity laying hold on truths which he has most certainly proved and valued for himself. What could be more reassuring than passages of God's Word such as *Romans 8*, and particularly verses 33-34?

> **'Who shall lay any thing to the charge of God's elect? It is God that justifieth. Who is he that condemneth? It is Christ that died.'**

When Satan throws his fiery darts of doubt we need only say: 'God has pronounced my justification in the court of Heaven, and this can never be undone; praise His glorious name!'

Pastorally, we must encourage the young particularly to praise more in their own devotions, for they have grown up in a 'gratitude-free' culture where all benefits are taken for granted, rendering them (as Christians) highly vulnerable to long-term assurance problems. Praise and thanksgiving are vital pillars of assurance, and a sympathetic pastor will constantly stress this.

Above all, praise must focus on Jesus Christ our Lord, and His unfailing power over Satan, the author and insinuator of seasons of diminished assurance. If feelings fail, praise Him in the darkest moments using only the intellect, for He will rescue His own from times of darkness. Isaac Watts put it so perfectly in his magnificent version of *Psalm 13*:–

How long wilt Thou conceal Thy face?
My God, how long delay?
When shall I feel those heavenly rays
That chase my fears away?

See how the prince of darkness tries
All his malicious arts:

He spreads a mist around my eyes,
And throws his fiery darts.

How would the tempter boast aloud
If I became his prey!
And how the sons of earth grow proud
At Thy so long delay.

But hell shall fly at Thy rebuke,
And Satan hide his head;
He knows the terrors of Thy look,
And hears Thy voice with dread.

Thou wilt display that sovereign grace
Where all my hopes have hung:
I shall employ my heart in praise,
And victory shall be sung.

If reflection on verses such as these does not begin to move a time of heaviness, then consider the wealth of affirmation in the Watts version of *Psalm 56*:–

God counts the sorrows of His saints,
Attends to all their prayers;
Tenderly follows our complaints,
And still records our tears.

When to Thy throne I raise my cry,
Then devils fear and flee,
So swift is prayer to reach the sky,
So near is God to me.

In Thee, most holy, just and true,
I have reposed my trust;
Nor will I fear what man can do,
Mere offspring of the dust.

As Thou hast vowed to bless me, Lord,
To Thee I'll yield my praise;
How good, how faithful is Thy Word;
How kind are all Thy ways.

Thou hast secured my soul from death;
Now free from sin I'd be,
That heart and hand, and life and breath,
May be employed for Thee.

The second scriptural category of assurance described in the confessions involves the recognition of inward evidence of salvation, and this also is brought to life by thanksgiving. The idea is not merely to observe God's work within us for self-gratification, but for thanksgiving to Him. We surely owe Him the praise for all that He has done *for us*, and *in us*. When we encourage young converts to see God's blessing in their lives we present the basic signs of conversion, six of which are conveniently to be found in *Acts 2*. (These are set out in the writer's booklet *Seven Certain Signs** and summarised at the end of this chapter under the heading – *Assurance and New Believers.*)

Seasoned believers have many indications of God's work within them stretching back over many years, and should be humbled and encouraged by the evidences of the lordship of Christ in their lives. They will certainly see themselves as disobedient to God in many ways, but if they have an active conscience and a strong desire and longing to obey, they should certainly conclude that these have been put within them by the Spirit of God working in their hearts. Also, if the Word of God exercises a powerful authority in our lives, and we desire to obey Christ first and foremost, this observation should move us to gratitude. Despite our unworthiness, the struggle and desire to please Him are authentic signs of life. Has the work of the Spirit made us people of prayer who feel impoverished, empty and even unclean when we fail to pray? Love for Christ is another evidence of grace, as Paul shows in *1 Corinthians 13.*

Proof that a process of sanctification has been started in us is apparent from our possessing an instinctive opposition to personal sin, so that whether we succeed or fail in holiness we hate our sin more than we love it, and we are ashamed of it.

Is it wholesome to be taking satisfaction from inward graces? May

**Seven Certain Signs of True Conversion*, Peter Masters, Sword & Trowel Booklet, London, 1994; ISBN 1 899046 05 4.

this not induce pride and self-satisfaction? The answer is that the observation of inward grace should never provoke pride because we will also see so much which is grievous and humbling. But will we become introspective by examining evidence of inward grace? It is possible, but not if our overriding purpose is to pay our debt of praise to God, and if looking within for evidence is only a part of our effort to consolidate assurance. The evidence of answered prayer is more significant, especially when we are proving the Lord by commitment to His glad service.

The Witness of the Spirit and Prayer

Returning to the subject of prayer, this is a great evidence of grace and answers to prayer are notable strengtheners of certainty. In this book we have placed answers to prayer under the witness of the Spirit of adoption witnessing with our spirit, because it is a feature of God dealing with us as sons. The longer we live the greater becomes our memory-bank of divine provision, deliverance, overruling and intervention in our affairs, in answer to prayer. Connected with this is service for the Lord, for as we engage in Gospel work, in witness or Sunday School teaching or visitation or any other undertaking, we pray for help and strength, and receive the unmistakable blessing of God in so many ways. This unquestionably increases assurance, giving us much certainty and gladness. Believers lacking assurance are often uninvolved in service for the Lord; never stretched; seldom longing for souls, and never pressed beyond measure.

Answered prayer is a large part of the witness of the Spirit with our spirit. There are times when we simply cannot meet all the obligations of secular life *and* of the service of Christ, but the Lord enables us. As we seek to increase our zeal for the Lord's work and receive necessary strength in answer to prayer, assurance is given 'fuel' on which to flourish.

An important aspect of prayer is regular engagement in fervent intercessory prayer, firstly because concern for the souls and spiritual progress of others proves that we have been given something of the mind of Christ, and we are therefore 'partakers of the divine nature', and secondly, because wonderful answers come when backsliders are turned round or hearts of seemingly obdurate rebels bend to the Saviour. If we were to keep a list of people or situations over which we have interceded, we would see over time remarkable answers to prayer, and our own conviction and certainty would become almost unassailable by Satan.

At the risk of repeating matter covered under our review of texts, we emphasise the warning against taking a mystical view of the Holy Spirit's witness in assurance. The idea that special, direct, mystical effusions of the Spirit will lift believers up in soaring, ecstatic and sensational experiences of 'pure glory' is simply not in the Bible, unless introduced by the reader against the context. Since the Reformation some of the best teachers have spoken often of the powerful blessing of the Spirit in giving assurance to believers, testifying that on occasions they have personally experienced a sublime sense of God's majesty and Christ's incomparable love that has overwhelmed and uplifted them to a remarkable degree. But they have usually stressed that such blessings came to them while engaged in contemplation of the Word, when the Spirit enriched their understanding and appreciation of great truths. Elevated moments of spiritual assurance are not the normal and everyday experience of believers, and they are the same in essence as the regular work of the Spirit in touching the mind and heart to magnify the believer's appreciation of spiritual realities. The point for us is that we should never think in terms of directly imparted mystical or 'charismatic' sensations, but in terms of the Spirit witnessing with our own souls when these are engaged in such spiritual activities as biblical reflection, affirmation, praise and prayer. Assurance by the Spirit which comes by this route is *always* full of joy and peace, and *sometimes* very glorious.

Assurance and New Believers

We now return to the question of whether assurance is experienced immediately at the time of conversion. Most believers first hear the Gospel with doubt and resistance, perhaps even with resentment, then the Spirit works within, opening their eyes, inclining their will, and giving a deep sense of need and awareness of sin. It then seems obvious to them that the Gospel is true, so that however entrenched their former prejudices, doubts and antagonism, they realise that this message is vital for their souls. The facts of redemption are seen to be powerful and essential, and the new seeker grasps very clearly that the Saviour's death on Calvary is the only way of salvation. All this comes by the work of the Spirit – 'For by grace are ye saved through faith; and that not of yourselves: it is the gift of God' *(Ephesians 2.8).* This faith sees and is certain, and any doubts that remain are not so much about whether salvation is true, as whether *they* will be saved. This is now the chief stumbling block – can we be sure that the promises of salvation will apply in our case? We believe the Gospel, but can we be sure of our personal salvation?

We observe seekers who appear to have undergone this dramatic change in their understanding, concern, beliefs, and desire for Christ, and yet still cannot be sure they have been saved. They are convinced, and some biblical signs of conversion may be apparent, but still they have no assurance. They believe they have repented and appropriated the blessing, but the realisation and sense of being a Heaven-bound child of God has not yet dawned.

We cannot resolve the hidden things of the heart, and it may be that some crucial step of faith has not been taken. However, it could be, in the case of some, that a truly saved person recoils from presuming himself to be saved even after a great change of attitude has occurred, and this is where the second basis of assurance becomes helpful to him – the recognition of inward evidences of conversion.

If the seeker will recognise what has already taken place in his life, then he will no longer continue in perplexed doubt, denying the Lord the praise that is His due.

This unassured seeker wants no more of this vain world and longs to know that his sins are forgiven. He feels these things strongly and just needs a sight of the signs of God's grace already within him to unlock the blessing of assurance, and to release his praise to God. In the case of a person very earnestly longing for Christ, in whom the signs of salvation are clearly evident to onlookers, though not to himself, it may fall to spiritual shepherds to give encouragement by helping that person to see what the Lord has already done in his life. The basic signs are the following:

(1) There has been an unmistakable experience of a person having seen his spiritual lostness and condemnation, and conviction of sin, resulting in sincere repentance and dependence on Christ; the 'valley of conviction'.

(2) A new view of the Bible has dawned, and the person has submitted willingly to its light and supreme authority in his life.

(3) He has already gained a deep sense of the family bond, feeling a new and special kinship with fellow believers.

(4) He has discovered prayer and received real answers from the Lord.

(5) There is clear evidence of a changed heart, the person now having radically different interests, desires and concerns.

(6) An element of assurance has been gained, at least in the form of an instinctual certainty of the inspired nature of the Word and of the truth of the message of the Gospel, if not of personal salvation.

(7) The person has now felt the attacks of Satan, usually in terms of doubts and fears fired into the mind.

It may well be that an unassured but seemingly earnest seeker after Christ needs to learn that faith is not only the hand which embraces and appropriates salvation, but also the hand that keeps hold on

Christ subsequently. The young believer's assignment is – faith! It is his duty and obligation, and also the source of his assurance. So, in conformity to the Scriptures we should help converts to see that assurance flows firstly from continuing faith in the promises of the Gospel, secondly from appreciation (with thanksgiving) of the evidences of grace within, and thirdly from the answers that flow from earnest prayer.

11

Assurance and the Unpardonable Sin

'If any man see his brother sin a sin which is not unto death, he shall ask, and he shall give him life for them that sin not unto death. There is a sin unto death: I do not say that he shall pray for it' *(1 John 5.16).*

THE UNPARDONABLE SIN – the sin of blasphemy against the Holy Spirit – is referred to in three Gospels, in *Hebrews 6.4-6*, and (possibly) *1 John 5.16*. Some very troubled believers feel that they may have committed the unpardonable sin and become shut out of all hope of eternal life. These friends should find comfort in scriptures like *John 10.27-29* which assert that converted people can never be lost, but such passages only lead them to think that they must be mistaken about their conversion. It is therefore important to show just what the unpardonable sin is in order to prove to anxious believers that they could not possibly have committed it. This sin is first referred to by the Lord in *Matthew 12.31-32*:–

> **'Wherefore I say unto you, All manner of sin and blasphemy shall be forgiven unto men: but the blasphemy against the Holy Ghost shall not be forgiven unto men. And whosoever speaketh a word against**

> **the Son of man, it shall be forgiven him: but whosoever speaketh against the Holy Ghost, it shall not be forgiven him, neither in this world, neither in the world to come.'**

The context of these verses is the Lord's healing of a demon-possessed person who was both blind and dumb. Those who witnessed the healing were amazed, exclaiming, 'Is not this the son of David?' but the Pharisees retorted, 'This fellow doth not cast out devils, but by Beelzebub the prince of the devils.' The Saviour, knowing their thoughts, exposed the unreasonableness of their slanderous remarks, and condemned them for their unpardonable sin.

His words were clearly directed at those who claimed He worked by an unclean spirit. He declared that all kinds of sin and blasphemy would be forgiven, including unbelief in Himself, but when that unbelief and slander came from people who were privileged to have witnessed His personal authentication by the power of the Holy Spirit, it became *unpardonable.* Many of the Pharisees who witnessed the miracles of Christ were not merely doubters, or those who slandered Him in ignorance, but eyewitnesses of astonishing miracles of healing. Yet they summoned all their obstinacy and hostility to deny everything they saw, suppressing any spiritual conviction, and rejecting the Lord's undeniable demonstration of divinity and glory. Furthermore, they fanned the flame of hatred in their hearts and spread the most insulting slanders possible, namely that Christ worked His miracles by the power of the devil. Their blasphemy was inexcusable because it involved the rejection of invincible and closely observed miracles.

According to the famous Scottish commentator David Brown the verses in *Matthew* make clear that blasphemy against the Holy Spirit was the sin of those who slandered the Saviour 'after the blaze of glory which the Holy Spirit threw around His claims, and in the full knowledge of all that' and who displayed 'a malignant determination to shut their eyes to all evidence'. It was never an unforgivable sin to oppose the Lord ignorantly, in unbelief (like

Paul in *1 Timothy 1.13*). Many hold that the unpardonable sin of blasphemy against the Holy Spirit could only be committed in the days that Christ walked on earth and during the time of apostolic signs and wonders. Certainly the Pharisees of *Matthew 12* witnessed scenes which have never been repeated since the time of Christ, for they saw Him in person displaying the full and irrefutable glory of divine power.

But supposing the unpardonable sin may still be committed today, what precisely would offenders do to be guilty of it? The words of *1 John 5.16* certainly suggest this possibility:–

> **'If any man see his brother sin a sin which is not unto death, he shall ask, and he shall give him life for them that sin not unto death. There is a sin unto death: I do not say that he shall pray for it.'**

Bearing in mind that this epistle dwells much on apostates, these being former church members who subsequently renounced Christ, we must conclude that these were the people who were committing the 'sin unto death'. After their denial of Christ they evidently became false teachers vehemently opposing Christ (mentioned in *1 John 4.1, 2.19*).

In *Hebrews 6.4-6* we learn more about people who have gone beyond redemption:–

> **'For it is impossible for those who were once enlightened, and have tasted of the heavenly gift, and were made partakers of the Holy Ghost, and have tasted the good word of God, and the powers of the world to come, if they shall fall away, to renew them again unto repentance; seeing they crucify to themselves the Son of God afresh, and put him to an open shame.'**

These one-time 'believers' apostatised totally and became so antagonistic as to 'crucify to themselves the Son of God afresh, and put him to an open shame'. Implacable and incapable of repentance they became bitter enemies of the faith, discrediting, injuring and ridiculing the name of Christ. This was obviously inspired by a deep hatred of the Lord coupled with a determined indifference to the state of their own souls and those of others. They did not do these things 'ignorantly in unbelief', but after having received a clear understanding of the faith, having professed conversion, and having seen evidence of the power of conversion in changing other lives *(Hebrews 6.4)*. Such apostates were not merely backsliders, but enemies and attackers of Christ's person and work.

Believers who fear that they have committed blasphemy against the Holy Spirit do not usually resemble these people in any respect. They do not hate Christ; they do not spurn the Truth; they do not slander and abuse the Saviour so as to bring Him to an open shame, and they do not attribute the work of the Spirit to the devil (as the Pharisees did). It is true that some believers are afflicted by horrible unwanted thoughts in which expressions of unbelief and slander come into their minds, but these are not their own free and voluntary thoughts and they long to be rid of them. The unpardonable sin is deliberate and resolute slander, openly expressed to convince others, and never regretted or repented of.

Nor is the unpardonable sin a period of backsliding, however sinful and unworthy that may be, and however much the backslider, while consumed by rebellion and insolence, may have blasphemed and denied the Lord. If the backsliding comes to an end so that the person becomes alarmed, mortified and repentant, there is forgiveness with the Lord. The unpardonable sin is of such intensity and so entrenched that the offender never repents. Backsliders, on repentance, may be forgiven as we see from God's appeal to backsliders in *Jeremiah 3.22*. *Hosea 14.4* is another promise of God to heal and love the backslider.* We may think also of Simon Peter's restoration after denying Christ. The unpardonable sinner, by contrast, never intends to repent, and never does.

* 'Return, ye backsliding children, and I will heal your backslidings. Behold, we come unto thee; for thou art the Lord our God' *(Jeremiah 3.22)*. 'I will heal their backsliding, I will love them freely: for mine anger is turned away from him' *(Hosea 14.4)*.

Believers who fear that they may have committed the unpardonable sin are not in this obdurate, determinedly unrepentant condition. They live in fear of the judgement of God, longing and anguishing for a consoling ray of assurance. Even if they have spent time as backsliders, they now believe in the Lord Jesus Christ with all their hearts, believing His every word, miracle and deed, and no longer would they intentionally shame or deride Him before the world, let alone ascribe His power to the devil. If they are contrite, their conduct or attitude does not correspond to that of people who are described in the Bible as having blasphemed against the Holy Spirit.

Sometimes a very unassured believer may see something of the rebelliousness and selfishness of his heart, recoiling in horror, and at that moment the devil makes that person feel he has sinned against light and blessing, has blasphemed against the Holy Spirit, and will never again have any grace from the hand of God. But Satan's charge cannot possibly be true in the case of a *concerned* person. The blasphemer against the Spirit is unconcerned, unafraid, and hardened in that condition. Such a person has an implacable hatred for Christ and is outside the range of tender convictions or of any pangs of conscience.

The believer who disobeys God in some matter, and who subsequently experiences an aching heart and fear of chastisement is certainly not the proud and hardened slanderer of *Matthew 12.31*. Even the believer who unworthily enters into contention with Christ after some divine chastisement is not like the Pharisees of that chapter, for such a person does not go so far as to renounce the faith and verbally discredit the Lord before the world.

To summarise, the believer who fears and respects God so much as to be deeply worried about having committed the unpardonable sin cannot possibly have done so. Such a person has too wounded a conscience, and totally lacks the settled cynical hatred required for this sin. Also, that person does not blatantly defame the Lord before the world. All these things are essential ingredients for the blasphemy against the Holy Spirit.

Finally, were the Pharisees of *Matthew 12* ever found meekly worshipping at the feet of Christ, waiting respectfully upon His teaching? Were the people of *Hebrews 6* who 'fell away' and who put Christ to 'an open shame', still seen worshipping among the people of God, longing for a blessing? Those who blasphemed against the Spirit in the Gospels, and the apostates referred to in *Hebrews 6* and *1 John 5*, were no longer worshippers of Christ, but had turned their backs on Christian worship and gone out of the churches. How can it be that those who still attend services are like those haters and slanderers of Christ? The person who is scared of having committed the unpardonable sin usually wants nothing more than peace with God and assurance of salvation. He certainly does not scorn Christ's deity and glory.

It is a witness only to the detestable subtlety of Satan that true believers, whose hearts long for a touch of God upon their lives, can become convinced that they have committed this ultimate wickedness against their Lord. How eager we should be to rescue them from this agonising mistake!

12

Feeling the Presence of the Lord

'The secret of the Lord is with them that fear him; and he will shew them his covenant' ***(Psalm 25.14).***

HOW EXACTLY DO BELIEVERS sense the presence of the Lord in their lives? Many passages of Scripture refer to a close union with Christ, including *Ephesians 3.19* where Paul prays that believers may 'know the love of Christ, which passeth knowledge', and that they may be 'filled with all the fulness of God'. In the *Psalms* there is a wide variety of expressions indicating the closeness of the Lord, such as *Psalm 140.13,* which speaks of how the upright shall dwell in the Lord's presence, and *Psalm 91.1* which breathes wonderful intimacy in the promise – 'He that dwelleth in the secret place of the most High shall abide under the shadow of the Almighty.'

In his hour of repentance, David prayed: 'Cast me not away from thy presence' *(Psalm 51.11). Psalm 25.14* has the striking expression 'the secret of the Lord' to describe union with God, the Hebrew word referring to a close-knit gathering or a 'session' in which people closely confer in a confidential setting.

All this raises a problem, for how is such closeness to be sensed? If believers do not know the answer to this question they are vulnerable to the mystical and sensational ideas of the charismatic movement, and to the imagined experiences of pietistic and 'higher life' teachers. What, then, is this secret presence or closeness of the Lord? Is it a feeling? And if it is a feeling, what kind of feeling is in mind – a touch perhaps, or a tingling, or some other strange physical or emotional sensation? At the outset we must make clear that knowing the presence of the Lord is not a physical feeling. Of course, anyone who loves the Lord and experiences His interventions in his life will experience strong feelings of happiness, gratitude and gladness. Believers feel such emotions very deeply as they consider the things of the faith, but their actual union with the Lord is not perceived by any *physical* or *mystical* sensation.

Many earnest Christians have picked up this idea that they ought to be able to sense Christ directly by some mystical realisation of Him that goes beyond certainty, happiness and gratitude, but this is *pietism* not biblical Christianity. We cannot have any *tangible* feeling of God's presence, for the simple reason that we are to know this *by faith*, and this chapter will seek to show how this works and how we feel as the result. All spiritual experience is channelled through the mind as the things of Christ are contemplated and grasped, and all legitimate feelings are produced by way of response to what the mind appreciates. Without conscious understanding, the 'feelings-system' cannot properly respond (and some believers will consequently try to activate their feelings wrongly, by rhythmic music or sentimentality). As the believer grasps Truth and considers its wonders, the Holy Spirit brings these things into even clearer focus, stirring depths of wonder, love and praise, sometimes to a very elevated degree. But there is no such thing as a direct touch of God upon the feelings, by-passing the agency of the mind.

Some people think that they feel the very presence of God, and that imagined leadings, visions and words of knowledge springing into their minds are all evidence of the Lord's presence, but this is foolish and mistaken, and may even be a form of proud spiritual elitism. These things are no indication of the presence of the Lord. We must repeat, Scripture teaches that we know the presence of the Lord *by faith,* via the conscious mind, and not by the direct touch on body or emotions by the finger of God. Although we do not sense Him by tangible feeling, faith makes Him utterly certain to us, and our faith is further confirmed by the wonderful things that He does in our lives.

But how can I believe, say some, without a felt sensation, or a tingling or something else to provide an unmistakable supernatural proof of His nearness? We do not need this for (as we have seen in the chapters on assurance) as we believe and as we think about spiritual things the Spirit imparts to us a deep grasp of them, coupled with a great appreciation and solid certainty.

The 'secret of the Lord' in *Psalm 25* refers to His nearness to His people. What may we reflect on in order to develop our certainty and enjoyment of Christ's nearness *by faith*? The following paragraphs attempt to answer this question. In what sense is the Lord near to us?

1. In His View

First, the language of nearness tells us that *we are in His view* for He watches us all the time, and this is a powerfully uplifting and encouraging thought. Christ is near us as One Who regards us with great affection, and we must deeply appreciate this. We cannot feel His presence or see Him literally, but we are certain that He observes us constantly with delight because the Scripture teaches us so. He knows our situation through and through, and whatever happens to us is seen by Him, for He permits it to occur, and He is ready to help as we call upon Him. To be reminded of this daily is to know by faith that He is near, and to be mightily comforted and strengthened.

This realisation also increases our zeal for holiness, because if we truly grasp that He sees our every move, reads our every thought and hears our every word, we become far more concerned about our sin. The biggest curb upon godlessness in Christian people is this daily awareness that the Lord is, as it were, standing right next to us, not only with a kindly gaze, but sometimes also with a disciplinary frown. Imagined mystical sensations never helped anyone to make progress in character and behaviour, but to grasp Christ's nearness *by faith* has a strong curbing and refining effect.

2. Within Hearing Distance

Secondly, the concept of the Lord's nearness speaks of how easy it is to speak to Him. Is His presence a tangible touch or a feeling? No, rather it is the assurance that He hears every word we utter, including every thought, and is able to respond according to His wisdom. We do not pray to a God Who is a million miles away, but to One Who knows our situation as though standing alongside us. We cannot see Him or visualise Him, but the idea of His closeness helps us to pray, and in the right spirit, with reverence, realism and trust.

3. At Hand to Protect

Thirdly, the nearness of the Lord also reminds us of our inviolable security and protection, for how could we fall and be disastrously, eternally swept away in the very presence of an omnipotent Saviour? This awareness comforts the heart and strengthens faith, and while we may shamefully sin and dishonour the name of Christ, He is near and will discipline us, perhaps severely if necessary, and bring us back to a faithful walk. This security should not serve as an encouragement to sin, because the discipline of the Lord can be hard to bear, but spiritual security is confirmed to us when we realise that

Christ, being near, notes every danger, hurt, transgression and departure, and directs the processes of rescue, reclamation and restoration.

4. Near to Train

Fourthly, we remember that we have to be trained up in holiness and in effective service for the Lord, and for this purpose Christ's Spirit indwells us. It is not only a matter of keeping us eternally safe, but of our development as God's people, and the Saviour's nearness, by His Spirit, is richly illustrative. A top-flight sportsman cannot be trained unless his coach is present watching his every move, detecting what he does incorrectly, and sketching out fresh approaches to accomplish improvement. A coach must follow every action, analysing, correcting and motivating. The fact of Christ's nearness to His people illustrates His glorious efficiency in training us, designing situations to strengthen and to develop faith, prayer and forbearance. He looks at each believer and says, 'This child of Mine needs more patience, or more compassion, or greater understanding, or increased boldness,' and so He develops our graces for His glory.

As sportsmen must readily respond to a coach, so no believer may benefit from Christ's training without prayerful willingness to co-operate with the programme of the Lord. The nearness and presence of the Lord is not a *feeling*, but a *realisation* and a confidence that He has a purpose in directing and allowing everything that happens in our lives, all events being capable of correcting and developing Christian character. Paul Gerhardt's words show the trusting attitude of the believer who appreciates by faith the nearness of the Lord:

Leave to His sovereign sway
To choose and to command;
So shall you, wondering, own His way,
How wise, how strong His Hand!

5. Near to Help, Direct, and Remind

Fifthly, the presence of the Lord means that Christ is there to prompt us, by His Spirit, to remember our spiritual duties, to instruct us (from the Word), and to remind us of many vital duties in life. This is not to suggest that Christ speaks to us by way of revelation, because all the authoritative Truth of God is contained in His Holy Word, and revelation has ceased. The Spirit, however, will often bring into our minds something we have learned from the Word, sometimes, for example, prompting us when we are speaking for Him in personal witness, or helping us during private study of the Word. Praying Christians also experience occasions in their working day when they would have made a disastrous mistake or omission but suddenly their mind was jogged and the possible 'catastrophe' averted, because the Spirit stirred the mind putting the forgotten matter into view. He does not communicate authoritative Truth, except to remind us of what we have learned from the Word, but He does help us in all our ways, as we look to Him, intervening in our circumstances. The concept of nearness reminds us of this wonderful privilege.

6. Near to Stir Conscience

Sixthly, the concept of the Lord's nearness speaks of His work of conviction when a moment of temptation comes and we begin to yield to it. By His Spirit the Saviour sees and sounds the alarm, so that a chord is struck within the conscience and we know that we should not do that thing. His nearness keeps the conscience alive, sensitive, and reactive. If we do not co-operate with the stirrings of conscience but rush wilfully on in some sinful word or act, then He may withdraw His kindly cautions and allow us to plunge into sin, pain, loss, discipline, and sad regrets. But if we look to Him to help us in the walk of holiness, He is near in the sense that He is able to put that precious warning touch upon us whenever we are about to go wrong. The concept of nearness therefore points to the close interaction of Christ with His people in the pursuit of holiness.

7. A Personal Teacher of Truth

Seventhly, the nearness of the Lord tells us that He is near as we read the Bible and reflect on His work (by the Spirit), touching our minds and bringing light and appreciation. Often He amplifies our understanding, and our hearts are strangely and powerfully warmed as a better grasp of some great matter dawns. Sometimes as we go through our day the Lord will illuminate a scripture that is in the mind, because He is always ready as the teacher of His people to deepen our delight in spiritual truths. Obviously, we must be 'into the Scripture' as regular Bible readers for Christ to touch our hearts and bring the meaning home to us. He is near in the sense that He closely follows and rewards our contemplation of His Word.

8. Close by to Apply Our Witness

Eighthly, the nearness of the Lord means that He is always close at hand to use us in His service. What can we achieve if we speak to an unconverted person? We cannot turn the stubborn will and melt the stony heart, but as we speak, because Christ is near, He may work in that heart by His Spirit, impressing upon our hearer the authenticity of our witness, and moving the conscience. We do not have to wait for Him to come, for He is ever at hand. If we try to help or comfort a fellow believer, how can we be sure that our words will prove helpful? In answer to prayer, Christ is always near and will apply our words to the understanding and the heart, and make them fruitful. The concept of the nearness of Christ greatly helps us to trust His gracious power, clothing our work and witness with stronger faith.

Misunderstanding Nearness

It is a great shame that some believers miss the real meaning of the language of nearness, seeing it as a reference to felt sensation. We hear people speak of inner ecstasies, even of tingling in hands and limbs, as they sensationally feel the presence of Christ. We hear others describing an unimaginable level of peace and joy as the touch of God comes upon their hearts, as though these experiences are the direct witness of the Spirit toward them. But as we have already insisted, there is no direct touch in the Christian faith, for every valid spiritual experience is *by faith*, and channelled first through the conscious mind. The idea of feelings communicated by the direct touch of God comes from Eastern mysticism, whereas the Christian faith says that our 'feelings-system' responds to precious truths as they are appreciated in our minds.

It is sad when Christian people veer into semi-mystical views because they become slaves and victims of transient emotional peaks, plunging frequently into their associated troughs. We know the Lord's presence not by transient emotions, but by remembering the treasures of Christ in His Word, and from the many benefits experienced from Him day by day. Then, whether we are unemotional people or the most excitable in the world, we are powerfully strengthened and uplifted to great joy and peace by the contemplation and realisation of these things. True and valid feelings are *derived* from what we grasp with our minds, our clarity of view being wonderfully magnified by the Spirit as we contemplate spiritual Truth.

Are There Conditions for Nearness?

Returning to our list of ways in which the Lord is near to His people, how may we be sure that He will perform all these activities in our case? The answer is given in *Psalm 25*: 'The secret of the Lord is with them that fear him; and he will shew them his covenant.' The promise is conditional, for although Christ is always near in the sense that we are never out of His sight, He will not necessarily act towards us as though He is present. He will not always restrain our troubles, or keep us from falling into sin, or intervene in our lives, or answer our prayers, or train us, or prompt us, or convict us of sin, or impart assurance, or throw light on the Word, or even use us as instruments in His service, because all these activities of Christ are conditional, the condition being – 'The secret of the Lord is with them that fear him.' We must fear Him, which means reverence, respect and obey Him in the walk of holiness.

Another condition is: 'Lead me in thy truth, and teach me: for thou art the God of my salvation; on thee do I wait all the day' *(Psalm 25.5).* We must take seriously the study of the Word. Yet another condition is: 'The meek will he guide in judgment: and the meek will he teach his way' *(Psalm 25.9).* We must take guidance seriously, not flitting through life as though we were free to do whatever we like, but we should always remember we are bound to seek God's guidance in all our major decisions and follow the lifestyle set out in the Word.

A Daily Reflection for Believers

It is a tremendously elevating experience to appreciate that Christ is near *by faith* every day. We get up in the morning, go out to our business, and say to ourselves, 'Christ is near to me; He is watching me with great affection; He is ready to intervene in my affairs; He knows everything that is going to happen to me and will turn every situation to my eternal spiritual good, and to the blessing of others. The Lord is at hand to answer my prayers; indeed He is so near He can do anything that is needful instantly; He will train me and strengthen me for harder service, and therefore I will trust, honour and love Him with my whole heart.'

The presence of God is not a feeling but a realisation, a belief, a conviction which sees and values the implications of the concept of nearness. It is one of the most wonderfully rewarding beliefs of the Christian life. To remember and value these ministries of Christ to His people is worth ten thousand strange sensations. Surely we should pray daily that the Lord would bring the wonders of Christ and His work into view, write them on our hearts and minds, and then stir our emotions in an appreciation derived from what we see.

The apostle said, 'We walk by faith,' and he prayed, 'That Christ may dwell in your hearts by faith' *(2 Corinthians 5.7* and *Ephesians 3.17)*. It was in this spirit – seeking to maintain a clear awareness of Christ's nearness *by faith* – that Toplady penned his great verses on communion with the Lord:–

Lord, it is not life to live
If Thy presence Thou deny;
Lord, if Thou Thy presence give
'Tis no longer death to die:
Source and Giver of repose,
Only from Thy smile it flows;
Peace and happiness are Thine;
Mine they are, if Thou art mine.

Whilst I feel Thy love to me,
Every object teems with joy;
May I ever walk with Thee,
For 'tis bliss without alloy:
Let me but Thyself possess,
Total sum of happiness:
Perfect peace I then shall prove,
Heaven below and Heaven above.

Appendix

Trials – A Christian Perspective

THE CHRISTIAN LIFE is a life of great joy and blessing in the Lord, but as far as earthly circumstances are concerned, the Bible warns that Christian believers may know many burdens, difficulties, and illnesses, and even severe trials, as the following representative passages show.

John 16.33 – 'These things I have spoken unto you, that in me ye might have peace. In the world ye shall have tribulation: but be of good cheer; I have overcome the world.' As soon as one trial is over, another may come, but our great consolation is that Christ has already won the battle of salvation for His people, and one day He will end this age and take all His own to uninterrupted eternal glory.

Acts 14.22 records how Paul and Barnabas toured the churches – 'confirming the souls of the disciples, and exhorting them to continue in the faith, and that we must through much tribulation enter into the kingdom of God'.

Romans 5.3 – 'We glory in tribulations also: knowing that

tribulation worketh patience.' Believers see the incalculable spiritual value of trials great and small, for through them God sanctifies and builds them up in prayerfulness and patience. Paul therefore exhorts believers to be 'patient in tribulation; continuing instant in prayer' *(Romans 12.12).*

1 Corinthians 9.12 – 'If others be partakers of this power over you, are not we rather? Nevertheless we have not used this power; but suffer all things, lest we should hinder the gospel of Christ.' At Corinth Paul set aside his right to be supported in the ministry and endured the consequences so that there should be no suspicion of his motives, and the Gospel should not be injured. The messengers of the Cross are not given every comfort and convenience by the Lord.

2 Corinthians 1.3-7 – 'Blessed be God, even the Father of our Lord Jesus Christ, the Father of mercies, and the God of all comfort; who comforteth us in all our tribulation, that we may be able to comfort them which are in any trouble, by the comfort wherewith we ourselves are comforted of God. For as the sufferings of Christ abound in us, so our consolation also aboundeth by Christ. And whether we be afflicted, it is for your consolation and salvation, which is effectual in the enduring of the same sufferings which we also suffer: or whether we be comforted, it is for your consolation and salvation. And our hope of you is stedfast, knowing, that as ye are partakers of the sufferings, so shall ye be also of the consolation.' Sufferings are permitted because they lead us to seek blessing from God, and they are especially given to teachers and mature believers so that they may teach the way of true comfort to the next generation of God's people.

2 Corinthians 7.4-6 – 'I am exceeding joyful in all our tribulation. For, when we were come into Macedonia, our flesh had no rest, but we were troubled on every side; without were fightings, within were fears. Nevertheless God, that comforteth those that are cast down, comforted us.' Paul speaks here of unrelenting problems leading to his being almost completely overwhelmed, but when all seemed hopeless, great comfort was provided by the arrival of Titus. Paul makes no mention of numerous little signs and provisions alleviating his trials hour by hour, nor of extraordinary incidents perpetually smoothing his way and removing all difficulties.

Galatians 5.11 – 'And I, brethren, if I yet preach circumcision, why do I yet suffer persecution? then is the offence of the cross ceased.' The more earnestly we evangelise by preaching and personal witness, the more likely we shall be to suffer rejection on account of the 'offence of the cross'.

Philippians 1.29 – 'For unto you it is given in the behalf of Christ, not only to believe on him, but also to suffer for his sake.' Many believers are chosen by God to demonstrate God's goodness and power in their suffering.

Philippians 4.11-13 – 'Not that I speak in respect of want: for I have learned, in whatsoever state I am, therewith to be content. I know both how to be abased, and I know how to abound: every where and in all things I am instructed both to be full and to be hungry, both to abound and to suffer need. I can do all things through Christ which strengtheneth me.' What a contrast we find between the teaching of the Bible and the teaching of some preachers today! Here we read that we are often called to prove the power of the Lord through times of shortage and difficulty.

1 Thessalonians 3.2-4 – 'And sent Timotheus, our brother, and minister of God, and our fellowlabourer in the gospel of Christ, to establish you, and to comfort you concerning your faith: that no man should be moved by these afflictions: for yourselves know that we are appointed thereunto. For verily, when we were with you, we told you before that we should suffer tribulation; even as it came to pass, and ye know.' The Thessalonians had suffered great troubles, and Paul explains that all believers are appointed by God to witness to Him despite many difficulties.

2 Thessalonians 1.4-5 – 'So that we ourselves glory in you in the churches of God for your patience and faith in all your persecutions and tribulations that ye endure: which is a manifest token of the righteous judgment of God, that ye may be counted worthy of the kingdom of God, for which ye also suffer.' The patience and prayerfulness of the Thessalonians was a proof of their standing in the Lord. How different the atmosphere among them must have been from the 'small talk' about the stream of miniature 'miracles' claimed by some believers today!

1 Timothy 4.10-11 – 'For therefore we both labour and suffer reproach, because we trust in the living God . . . These things command and teach.' Hard work for the Lord, coupled with scorn, will be the lot of zealous believers.

2 Timothy 1.8 and *12* – 'Be not thou therefore ashamed of the testimony of our Lord, nor of me his prisoner: but be thou partaker of the afflictions of the gospel according to the power of God . . . For the which cause I also suffer these things: nevertheless I am not ashamed: for I know whom I have believed, and am persuaded that he is able to keep that which I have committed unto him against that day.' Bear a testimony, says Paul, even in hardship, by the help of the Lord, and keep in mind the great day when Christ will come.

2 Timothy 2.9-10 – 'Wherein I suffer trouble, as an evil doer, even unto bonds; but the word of God is not bound. Therefore I endure all things for the elect's sakes.' Who knows what trials and tribulations are hinted at in these few words! Paul saw the power of God in the upholding strength he was given to endure trials, and the mighty power of the Gospel in the lives of those who heard it. When he was bound in prison, jailors and soldiers would be converted, and through them slaves and members of the noble households. But Paul did not usually see prison bars fall from windows and earthquakes split open the walls, as at Philippi.

2 Timothy 2.12 and *3.12* – 'If we suffer, we shall also reign with him . . . Yea, and all that will live godly in Christ Jesus shall suffer persecution.' In every age, faithful disciples shall suffer in some shape or form. If there is *no* hardship of any kind it suggests there is no deep committedness to holy living and to Christ's great commission.

Hebrews 13.3 – 'Remember them that are in bonds, as bound with them; and them which suffer adversity, as being yourselves also in the body.' Many believers suffer particularly acutely for the Saviour, and others are to lift them up in prayer, and to provide for them whenever the opportunity arises.

1 Peter 3.14-15 – 'If ye suffer for righteousness' sake, happy are ye: and be not afraid of their terror, neither be troubled; but sanctify the Lord God in your hearts: and be ready always to give an answer to every man that asketh you a reason of the hope that is in you with meekness and fear.' Unfair treatment and hostility will often hurt, but believers are not to be dismayed or unduly disturbed by it. When it happens – 'Reverence Christ in your hearts', says Peter, 'and be ready to take every opportunity for witness.'

1 Peter 4.19 – 'Wherefore let them that suffer according to the will of God commit the keeping of their souls to him in well doing, as unto a faithful Creator.' Faithfulness rather than deliverance from trial will often be the pathway which God intends for His people, and on that pathway they will be most blessed.

Joshua's Conquest

Was it moral? What does it say to us today?

119 pages, paperback, ISBN 1 870855 46 9

Rooted and grounded in love for the Lord, Joshua was utterly faithful, wonderfully stable, and scrupulously obedient. The book of the Bible that bears his name is a magnificent anthology of events to challenge and inspire God's children in every age.

This is a book for reading, rather than a commentary. Its aim is to bring out the spiritual message of *Joshua* for today, and also to explain some of the 'problem' portions and passages which evoke questions on, for example, the morality of so much killing, and whether God was responsible for hardening the hearts of the Canaanites. In *Joshua* we find the holiness and mercy of God fully displayed, and numerous encouragements for the spiritual life.

The Mutual Love of Christ and His People

An explanation of the *Song of Solomon* for personal devotions and Bible study groups

115 pages, paperback, ISBN 1 870855 40 X

The courtship of the *Song of Solomon* provides fascinating scenes and events designed to show the love of Christ for His redeemed people, and theirs for Him. Here, also, are lessons for Christians when they become cold or backslidden, showing the way to recover Christ's presence in their lives.

Prophecies of Christ abound in the *Song*, together with views of the bride's destiny, as she prepares to cross the mountains into eternal glory, where the greatest wedding of all will take place.

This book begins with a brief overview of the reasons why the *Song* should be seen as allegorical – the viewpoint held throughout church history by the overwhelming majority of preachers and commentators. Then, in verse-by-verse mode, but designed for continuous devotional reading, the symbols are explained and applied.

Testimonies to the blessing obtained through this treatment of the *Song* have come from all over the world, from ministers and 'lay' people alike.

God's Rules for Holiness

Unlocking the Ten Commandments

139 pages, paperback, ISBN 1 870855 37 X

Taken at face value the Ten Commandments are binding on all people, and will guard the way to Heaven, so that evil will never spoil its glory and purity. But the Commandments are far greater than their surface meaning, as this book shows.

They challenge us as Christians on a still wider range of sinful deeds and attitudes. They provide positive virtues as goals. And they give immense help for staying close to the Lord in our walk and worship.

The Commandments are vital for godly living and for greater blessing, but we need to enter into the panoramic view they provide for the standards and goals for redeemed people.

The Lord's Pattern for Prayer

118 pages, paperback, ISBN 1 870855 36 1

Subtitled – 'Studying the lessons and spiritual encouragements in the most famous of all prayers.' This volume is almost a manual on prayer, providing a real spur to the devotional life. The Lord's own plan and agenda for prayer – carefully amplified – takes us into the presence of the Father, to prove the privileges and power of God's promises to those who pray.

Chapters cover each petition in the Lord's Prayer. Here, too, are sections on remedies for problems in prayer, how to intercede for others, the reasons why God keeps us waiting for answers, and the nature of the prayer of faith.

Heritage of Evidence

127 pages, illustrated, paperback, ISBN 1 870855 39 6

In today's atheistic climate most people have no idea how much powerful evidence exists for the literal accuracy and authenticity of the biblical record. The British Museum holds a huge number of major discoveries that provide direct corroboration and background confirmation for an immense sweep of Bible history. This survey of Bible-authenticating exhibits has been designed as a guide for visitors, and also to give pleasure and interest to readers unable to tour the galleries. It will also be most suitable for people who need to see the accuracy and inspiration of the Bible.

The 'tour' followed here started life over forty years ago and has been used by many thousands of people including youth and student groups.

Almost every item viewed on the tour receives a full colour photograph. Room plans are provided for every gallery visited showing the precise location of artefacts, and time-charts relate the items to contemporary kings and prophets. The book is enriched by pictures and descriptions of famous 'proofs' in other museums.

Not Like Any Other Book

161 pages, paperback, ISBN 1 870855 43 4

Faulty Bible interpretation lies at the root of every major mistake and 'ism' assailing churches today, and countless Christians are asking for the old, traditional and proven way of handling the Bible to be spelled out plainly.

A new approach to interpretation has also gripped many evangelical seminaries and Bible colleges, an approach based on the ideas of unbelieving critics, stripping the Bible of God's message, and leaving pastors impoverished in their preaching.

This book reveals what is happening, providing many brief examples of right and wrong interpretation. The author shows that the Bible includes its own rules of interpretation, and every believer should know what these are.

Physicians of Souls

The Gospel Ministry

285 pages, paperback, ISBN 1 870855 34 5

'Compelling, convicting, persuasive preaching, revealing God's mercy and redemption to dying souls, is seldom heard today. The noblest art ever granted to our fallen human race has almost disappeared.'

Even where the free offer of the Gospel is treasured in principle, regular evangelistic preaching has become a rarity, contends the author. These pages tackle the inhibitions, theological and practical, and provide powerful encouragement for physicians of souls to preach the Gospel. A vital anatomy or order of conversion is supplied with advice for counselling seekers.

The author shows how passages for evangelistic persuasion may be selected and prepared. He also challenges modern church growth techniques, showing the superiority of direct proclamation. These and other key topics make up a complete guide to soul-winning.

Worship in the Melting Pot

148 pages, paperback, ISBN 1 870855 33 7

'Worship is truly in the melting pot,' says the author. 'A new style of praise has swept into evangelical life shaking to the foundations traditional concepts and attitudes.' How should we react? Is it all just a matter of taste and age? Will churches be helped, or changed beyond recognition?

This book presents four essential principles which Jesus Christ laid down for worship, and by which every new idea must be judged.

Here also is a fascinating view of how they worshipped in Bible times, including their rules for the use of instruments, and the question is answered – What does the Bible teach about the content and order of a service of worship today?

Men of Purpose

157 pages, illustrated, paperback, ISBN 1 870855 41 8

This book brings into one illustrated volume eleven great lives, all with an experience of personal conversion to God. Composer Mendelssohn, food industrialist Henry Heinz, novelist Daniel Defoe, and some of the most celebrated scientists of all time, are among the examples of leading people whose lives were changed by a sight of real Christianity. Also very suitable as a gift to unconverted friends, and to enrich sermons and Bible class messages.

Do We Have a Policy?
For church health and growth
93 pages, paperback, ISBN 1 870855 30 2

Only One Baptism of the Holy Spirit
109 pages, paperback, ISBN 1 870855 17 5

The Healing Epidemic
227 pages, paperback, ISBN 1 870855 00 0

The Charismatic Phenomenon *[co-authored with John C. Whitcomb]*
113 pages, paperback, ISBN 1 870855 01 9

Steps for Guidance
184 pages, paperback, ISBN 1 870855 19 1

Biblical Strategies for Witness
126 pages, paperback, ISBN 1 870855 18 3

Should Christians Drink?
112 pages, paperback, ISBN 1 870855 12 4

www.wakemantrust.org